Parliamentary Enclosure in England
An Introduction to its Causes, Incidence
and Impact 1750–1850

Parliamentary Enclosure in England

*An Introduction to its Causes, Incidence
and Impact 1750–1850*

G.E. MINGAY

Longman
London and New York

Addison Wesley Longman Limited Edinburgh Gate,
Harlow, Essex CM20 2JE, United Kingdom
and Associated Companies throughout the world.

*Published in the United States of America
by Addison Wesley Longman, New York.*

First published 1997

ISBN 0–582–25726–3 CSD
ISBN 0–582–25725–5 PPR

British Library Cataloguing in Publication Data

A catalogue entry for this title is available from the British Library

Library of Congress Cataloging-in-Publication Data

Mingay, G.E.
Parliamentary enclosure in England : an introduction to its
causes, incidence, and impact, 1750–1850 / G.E. Mingay.
p.   cm.
Includes bibliographical references and index.
ISBN 0–582–25726–3 (csd). — ISBN 0–582–25725–5 (ppr)
1. Inclosures—England—History.   2. Inclosures—Government
policy—England—History.   I. Title.
HD594.6.M533   1998
33.2—dc21   97–25200
CIP

Set by 35 in 10/12pt Baskerville
Produced by Longman Singapore Publishers (Pte) Ltd.
Printed in Singapore

Contents

Acknowledgements

This book could not have been written without the assistance of the numerous archivists who over many years provided me with a wealth of original sources. The author has benefited greatly from conversations with Dr John Chapman of the University of Portsmouth, who kindly read the first draft. Professor Alan Armstrong of the University of Kent was also kind enough to read the whole, and offered many valuable suggestions and improvements.

Maps 1 and 2 have been adapted by kind permission of Dawson UK Ltd (Archon Books), and Maps 3 and 4 have been reprinted by permission of Mr Rex C. Russell.

Lastly, the author must record his debt to the late Professor J.D. Chambers, who many years ago stimulated a lasting interest in the subject.

In references place of publication is London unless specified otherwise.

CHAPTER ONE

Introduction

Towards the close of the nineteenth century there was an upsurge of public interest in matters concerning the countryside. Some of this new attention was due to economic circumstances, arising especially from the depression which affected much of English farming in the last quarter of the century. But other elements had a social origin, centring on the conditions, particularly the housing, of the farm-worker, his poor living standards, his complete dependence on his low wages, his lack of education and, generally, lack of prospects. Contemporary observers could not help but notice the fact that the agrarian structure of England was markedly different from that which dominated large parts of continental Europe. The publication of the first comprehensive statistics on English farming reinforced the observation, and curiosity was stimulated into why the 'peasant' or small family farmer was relatively scarce over large areas of the English countryside.

The concern with a 'lost peasantry' was always somewhat exaggerated, for the enquiries made in 1887 and subsequent years showed that between 15 and 16 per cent of the cultivated land of England was still occupied by its owners. A more relevant figure, however, allowing for farms that because of the depression had fallen into the hands of their large owners, and allowing also for accommodation land kept by non-farming owners, was probably not above 12 per cent. The holdings statistics for 1885 were also revealing, showing that small farms of between 5 and 50 acres numbered over 200,000, and accounted for 14 per cent of the 27,700,000 acres reported on in England and Wales.[1] Small farmers, even small

1. J.H. Clapham, *Economic History of Modern Britain*, II, Cambridge, 1932, pp. 260–1, 264.

owner-farmers, had evidently not 'disappeared', though perhaps it was true that they were fewer than in the past. In the 1880s historical knowledge was too limited for even an approximate answer to be given on this point.

Whatever the facts, political and social motives inspired a number of published works dealing with various aspects of the later nineteenth-century village. Some were concerned with the continued domination of large landowners, some with farm-workers' conditions, and others with smallholdings – a rather vain attempt to restore a peasant class to the contemporary countryside. Best known, and most soundly based, perhaps, were Seebohm Rowntree and May Kendall's, *How the Labourer Lives* (1913), together with the detailed survey of the (Liberal) Land Enquiry Committee, *The Land,* of the same year, and the response of the Land Agents' Society, *Facts about Land,* of 1916.[2]

The academic strand of the controversy was primarily concerned with establishing when and how the small farmer had declined, with some historians concentrating on the period of the sixteenth and seventeenth centuries, and others on the age of the parliamentary enclosures. Among the major works were Gilbert Slater's *The English Peasantry and the Enclosure of Common Fields* (1907), Wilhelm Hasbach's *History of the Agricultural Labourer* (English translation, 1908), A.H. Johnson's *The Disappearance of the Small Landowner* (1909), R.H. Tawney's *The Agrarian Problem in the Sixteenth Century* (1912), and E.C.K. Gonner's *Common Land and Inclosure* (1912). Some of these books, notably those by Slater and Hasbach, followed a left-wing approach to the subject emanating from Marx's view of enclosure as the agency creating a landless industrial proletariat. The works by Johnson, Tawney and Gonner, it might be said, were more balanced interpretations of available evidence.

However, undoubtedly the most widely read and influential book was that by J.L. and Barbara Hammond, *The Village Labourer* of 1911.[3] The Hammonds in their work largely ignored other contemporary studies, and continued to do so in their later editions. It was they who established the generally accepted view of parliamentary enclosure as not only the cause of the dispossession of the peasantry but also the root cause of the rural poverty and unrest of

2. Seebohm Rowntree and May Kendall, *How the Labourer Lives: Study of the Rural Labour Problem,* 1913; Land Enquiry Committee, *The Land: the Report of the Land Enquiry Committee,* 1913; Land Agents' Society, *Facts about Land: A Reply to 'The Land',* the Report of the Unofficial Land Enquiry Committee, 1916.

3. J.L. and Barbara Hammond, *The Village Labourer,* 1st edn, 1911, new edn, 1978.

the period. Certainly they produced a highly readable study, even if their method was somewhat flawed: in particular, they noted, but then neglected, the significance of the limited area affected by parliamentary enclosure, and they failed to observe Gonner's approach in refusing to formulate simple generalisations. He purposely abstained, as he wrote, 'from dwelling at length on the incidents of a few cases. Such a method, while it may make things more picturesque, is misleading when the instances are few out of many thousands, and not necessarily typical.'[4]

However, such was the influence of the Hammonds' book that for long the orthodox view of parliamentary enclosure was that it was responsible for the major social problems of the later eighteenth- and early nineteenth-century countryside. Gonner's work, though in sobering contrast to that of the Hammonds, and also Johnson's earlier book, made little impact on this orthodoxy, in large part because neither work was well known outside academic circles. Later attacks on the Hammonds' position, from Sir John Clapham in the 1920s and Professor J.D. Chambers in subsequent years, also failed to weaken the Hammond orthodoxy, except in some degree at the rarefied level of the learned journals and university teaching.[5] And it is at this level, primarily, that the controversy has continued: between those who with the benefit of more recent research continue to support a somewhat modified Hammond position, and those who, again with the advantage of greater knowledge, expand on a modified Clapham/Chambers stance.

The present writer has tried to take a middle view, holding with Sir Edward Gonner that the subject is much too complicated to make simple generalisations valid. In particular, it is felt that one must dissect the rural society of the period into its component elements – large landowners, large farmers, owner-occupiers, small tenant farmers, and very small occupiers and cottagers – and consider the likely effects on each. To do this it is necessary to establish, so far as is possible, the facts of the pre-enclosure countryside, eschewing any romantic view of the life of the open fields and commons. For example, it is true that many commons did yield a variety of valuable resources for those having access to them, but a lager number of commons were of lesser value, some of little value, or none at all. And of course it has to be borne in mind that use of

4. E.C.K. Gonner, *Common Land and Inclosure*, 1st edn, 1912, preface, p. vii.
5. Clapham, *Modern Britain*, I, Cambridge, 1926, ch. iv; J.D. Chambers, 'Enclosure and Labour Supply in the Industrial Revolution', *Economic History Review*, 2nd ser., V, 3, 1953, pp. 319–43.

even the best of commons, for grazing, gathering fuel, and searching for berries and medicinal herbs, was extremely time-consuming.

Moreover, it was not only the commons which differed from parish to parish. Wide variations were found also in the size and number of the open fields and the method of their working; the soil might be a difficult one that was slow and expensive to work in terms of the rate of ploughing and the strength of the teams required; pasture might be good or poor, plentiful or scarce; and the villagers were involved in numerous disputes, for instance over the maintaining of drains, the depredations of insecurely tethered livestock, overstocking of the commons, encroachments on the uncultivated land, and the shrinkage of the open fields through piecemeal enclosure. Such wide variations in conditions reinforce Gonner's point: generalisation is far from easy, and should not be based on a handful of examples. To give concrete expression to this variety the present writer has drawn on a substantial body of documentary material as well as on published sources, and it is hoped that this will keep the complexity of the subject to the fore of the reader's mind.

Of course, parliamentary enclosure, affecting both property and customary rights as it did, and frequently in a major way, inevitably gave rise to friction, discontent, even violence. The disturbance of established property, and its enjoyment, has always been a source of conflict and remains so today: witness the opposition stirred up by major road improvement schemes or, most recently, the building of a Channel tunnel railway link across Kent.

In time the problems caused by parliamentary enclosure passed away, as the generations immediately affected by it receded, although it is certainly remarkable how long a folk-memory persisted, with late-nineteenth-century country people inclined to look back to a supposed golden age existing 'before the enclosure'. What has not so far disappeared are the changes wrought by enclosure on the landscape. Contemporaries were divided on the aesthetics of these changes, some feeling that the new lines of hedges, rectangular fields and straight, wide roads were offensive to the eye (and certainly less convenient for hunting), while others shed no tears for the extinction of the great expanses of open fields and broad, unkempt commons which to them seemed eyesores.

The landscape changes were indeed very remarkable, and noticeably so even today. There are parts of Lincolnshire, for example, where one can readily recognise the work of the enclosure Commissioners and their surveyors, particularly in the neatness of the field divisions and the straight roads, wide with edges of grass strips, roads which do not bend but change direction with sharp turns of ninety degrees. Owing to the requirements of the post-enclosure farmers, the fields on similar soils assumed a high degree of similarity, as Frank Emery points out. In areas where stone was readily available, dry-stone walls replaced the quickset hedges most commonly seen in the Midlands, and as open land was replaced by cultivated fields and new substantial farmhouses and cottages appeared, the centre of a community might find itself pulled away from its former position. Some consequences were often unwelcome: near Oxford, for example, the disappearance of the commons, it was complained, inhibited riding, prevented the pursuit of natural history, and cut off the university's students from fresh air. The former pretty, winding trackways were replaced by 'dull and dusty' footpaths along the newly made, formally direct roads. Apart from the many new country roads created by the Commissioners, the landscape was changed also by the incursions into woodlands necessary for obtaining the great quantities of timber required by landowners for their miles of new fences and numerous gates and gate-posts – a work which gave employment to a host of woodmen and carpenters, as well as to hedgers and ditchers, masons and roadmen.[6]

In northern England the proliferation of dry-stone walls and earthen banks subdividing newly enclosed waste lands completely altered the landscape, though where the land was too poor to bear the cost of making permanent divisions these might well be omitted. Again, in the Pennine valleys where minerals were to be found, small pieces of waste were enclosed by walls in order to provide some agricultural income for the miners and their families. Old woodland areas like Staffordshire's Needwood Forest, Leicestershire's Charnwood Forest and Dorset's Vale of Blackmoor were cleared and replaced by a pattern of geometrical fields and straight roads. The Lincolnshire wolds and the chalklands of Wiltshire, Dorset, Hampshire and Sussex also succumbed to the Commissioners' surveyors, although some parishes were enclosed by agreement among the owners rather than by Act of Parliament. A similar picture emerged in fenland districts, in the Somerset Levels for example, and the East Anglian fens, with innumerable rectangular fields edged by new straight drains replacing the old undrained fields and commons. And just as the new farmsteads sometimes took their names from contemporary events – Trafalgar Farm, Waterloo Farm – so

6. Frank Emery, *The Oxfordshire Landscape*, 1974, pp. 138, 140–3.

some of the new fields were called after the recently lost open fields and commons, or by more precise if mundane descriptions such as Twenty Acres or Fourteen Acres. The new crops introduced in the period were also commemorated by names such as Trefoil Close, Turnip Close, Potato Ground.[7]

So enclosure has left its marks, which are still evident some two centuries or more after the event. A present-day historian was once heard to remark that, as a subject for fresh discussion, enclosure was dead and buried. Nothing could be further from the truth. It continues to fascinate a younger generation of historians, as evidenced by the frequent appearance of important new research in books and articles. It is a subject, in fact, which has always aroused controversy and seems likely to continue to do so in the future. But too often, in the view of the present writer, the controversies are obscured by an unfortunate lack of balance and a failure to recognise the facts of the matter. If this book goes some way towards creating a more realistic basis for discussion, then the many years spent in bringing its material together will have been well used.

7. Christopher Taylor, *Fields in the English Landscape*, 1975, pp. 141, 143, 144, 146, 150, 152.

CHAPTER TWO

The Anatomy of Enclosure

The meaning of enclosure

What exactly was enclosure? What did it involve? Most simply, it meant the extinction of common rights which people held over the farm lands and commons of the parish, the abolition of the scattered holdings in the open fields and a re-allocation of holdings in compact blocks, accompanied usually by the physical separation of the newly created fields and closes by the erection of fences, hedges or stone walls. Thereafter, the lands so enclosed were held 'in severalty', that is, they were reserved for the sole use of the individual owners or their tenants.

What were the common rights that were extinguished by enclosure? We shall consider them in more detail later on, but broadly they were old-established rights exercised by the occupiers of farm lands and cottages, and varied considerably in nature and extent from place to place. Generally, however, on arable lands of the open fields they included the important right ('common of shack') to graze livestock on the corn stubbles left after the crops had been harvested and cleared from the ground. The manure dropped by the grazing stock was a vital element in securing satisfactory yields of following crops. Equally valuable was that provided by the systematic folding of sheep on the land that was left fallow, or uncultivated, between crops (left so in order to help it recover fertility and to allow for a thorough extermination of weeds). In addition to the open-field lands that were regularly cropped, there were in many unenclosed villages useful areas of meadow, perhaps enriched by a stream which flooded in winter. The meadows were highly valued for their early bite of rich grass, and not infrequently they were newly re-allocated each year, so that each farmer had an equal chance of access to the best grazing.

The common or commons (there might be more than one in the parish) consisted of areas of open land set aside for grazing during the summer months when the arable or crop lands in the fields were shut up to keep stock from damaging the growing corn. In addition to the farmers, numbers of cottagers and others might have the right to graze a cow or horse on the commons, find pannage (acorns and beech-mast) there for pigs, cut brushwood or furze for fuel, and gather berries and herbs in season. Contemporaries also spoke of the 'waste', a term which included small areas of stony or rocky ground together with more extensive stretches of heathland, moors and bogs, as well as barren mountains and steep hillsides. Parts of the waste might be useful for some very sparse grazing, for gathering wild berries and digging turves or peat for fuel, and perhaps for getting supplies of clay, gravel and stone for repairing houses and maintaining the roads.

Waste lands were often quite limited in lowland parishes but were very extensive over much of the country in the eighteenth century, even beyond the limits of the northern moors, the Cumbrian fells and the Welsh mountains. In the south-west, for example, lay the wastes of Dartmoor, Exmoor and Sedgmoor, in the Midlands were the bleak wolds and considerable areas of poor soils taken up by the royal and other forests, while in the east stretched the forbidding Lincolnshire uplands, the still ill-drained fenlands further south, and the Thames-side marshes. Even in approaching the capital itself, the traveller had to brave the highwaymen who infested wastes such as Hounslow Heath and Finchley Common. Some areas of hill and moor, especially in the north, were so high, steep and barren as never to be worth the cost of enclosing. But often unenclosed lowland parishes had some small patches of very poor land of such marginal value that they might not be worth taking in when the parish was enclosed, unless it were for their stone or minerals. Indeed, in lowland farming districts not only some wastes, but also a number of commons, remained untouched by enclosure, so that it is not quite true to say that the commons always disappeared along with the open fields.

Lastly, the parish often had some woodlands. These were usually privately owned and cultivated on a commercial basis, the trees being cut at regular intervals and systematically replanted. The large timber went for house building and shipbuilding, or to workshops making a variety of wooden articles such as furniture, posts, gates and wagon wheels, among many others, with the bark sold separately for use in the tanning trade, while coppice wood was used for making charcoal.

The arable land of the parish was frequently divided into a number of large fields. These have usually been described in historical accounts and in nineteenth-century General Enclosure Acts as 'open' fields, to distinguish them from enclosed ones. In reality, as Joan Thirsk has pointed out, there were two kinds of unenclosed fields. Firstly, there were fields where common rights are not definitely known to have been used, or where the farmers agreed to renounce them. Secondly, there were the fields where common rights had always existed and were still in use at the time of parliamentary enclosure. She suggested reserving the term 'open' fields for the first, and 'common' fields for the second, a distinction which in terms of historical accuracy has much to recommend it.[1] However, the use of 'open' fields to describe unenclosed arable fields in general is so long enshrined in the historical literature that to avoid confusion it is perhaps best to retain this term, while remembering that there were fields that were 'open' in a landscape sense but were not subject to common rights.

The number of fields varied from parish to parish, and although textbooks speak of the 'three-field system', and in fact three fields may have been quite usual, it was not uncommon to find parishes with only one or two fields and others with from four to seven or more. In the so-called 'classical' open-field system of the Midlands the fields were often large, stretching from several hundred acres to as many as two thousand acres or more; in some areas, on the other hand, they were quite small, the arable being subordinate to a predominating demand for grazing, or limited by the restricted availability of suitable soils. On the coast of Lincolnshire, for example, the salt marshes were highly valued for their pasture, and the small arable fields there were quite a secondary consideration.[2]

Whether the open fields formed a rigid basis for the rotation of crops, as was often supposed, is highly doubtful. Already by the later seventeenth century or early eighteenth century open-field farmers were experimenting with new crops, such as turnips and legumes.[3]

1. Joan Thirsk, ed., *The Agrarian History of England and Wales, IV: 1500–1640*, Cambridge, 1967, pp. ix–x.
2. Joan Thirsk, *English Peasant Farming: the Agrarian History of Lincolnshire from Tudor to Recent Times*, 1957, pp. 68, 152.
3. See, for example, Michael Havinden, 'Agricultural Progress in Open-field Oxfordshire', *Agricultural History Review*, IX, 1961, pp. 78–83.

Such crops were particularly useful to farmers where the commons were small and grazing was short, enabling them to keep more stock than would otherwise have been possible, and consequently helping them to manure their cropland more thoroughly. To some extent this flexibility made it possible for open-field farmers to overcome the basic weakness of their farming system – the more or less fixed division of the village land into that reserved for arable and that reserved for pasture. But clearly the new crops were not a universal panacea since their adoption was limited by the nature of the soils. Ill-drained clays, in particular, were unsuitable for roots or legumes, and so the enclosure of these soils, widespread in the Midlands, often resulted in no change in the basic system: two crops and a fallow continued to be the regime after enclosure as before. Further, since the claylands (unless adequately drained) were often also unsuited for conversion to pasture, and were difficult and costly to cultivate for corn crops, enclosing them was less profitable than with more amenable soils, and tended to be delayed. Again, the human factor might be important also. The conservatism of some open-field farmers meant a rooted antipathy to new ideas, however advantageous they might be. As a result, where new crops were not introduced, the commons were too small to allow all the farmers and cottagers to keep as many animals as they wished, and the arable was too 'worn out', that is, inadequately fertilised to bear good crops, this farming impasse became one of the more important arguments for enclosing.

As is well known, the holding of an individual farmer was often scattered in small areas or 'strips' across the open fields, an obvious source of inefficiency. The moving of teams and implements from strip to strip was time-consuming, and meant that part of the land in the fields had to be left unploughed in order to provide access. Further, the existence of so many different farmers' boundaries within a field gave occasion for encroachment and damage, accidental or otherwise, and was a fertile source of disputes. And since the farmhouses were usually grouped together in the centre of the village, or in a number of separate hamlets, time and effort had to be spent in journeying out to distant parcels of the holding which, in some instances might well lie at a distance of a mile or even two miles.

As it happened, the open fields had largely gone by the time that factory-made, horse-drawn field machines were coming widely into use in the second quarter of the nineteenth century, so the scattering of the holdings did not constitute an obstacle to making use of new economies of scale. Nevertheless, long before this, the inconvenience of holdings scattered in numerous small parcels had led to amalgamation and consolidation, sometimes on a large scale. More frequently, perhaps, individual farmers agreed to exchanges, so that over time the separate units in the fields got fewer and larger, and became easier to work. However, in numbers of villages before enclosure many of the units making up a holding were still very small, sometimes only a quarter of an acre, and still widely scattered, and this was frequently given as a ground for bringing about an enclosure.

Forms of enclosure

This book is primarily concerned with parliamentary enclosures, that is, those carried out under the authority of the private Acts of enclosure which accounted for the major, if uncertain, part of all the land enclosed over the period 1750–1830. However, there were two other important forms of enclosure that we must notice, enclosures that were carried out without the intervention of a private Act of Parliament.

The first of these is large-scale enclosures carried out by the common consent of the owners of the land, and known therefore as 'enclosures by agreement'. In this form of enclosure the owners in a parish agreed among themselves to enclose a large part or all of the fields and commons, together with any waste worth cultivating, and to allot the land in separate compact farms in proportion to the acreage, in quantity and value, originally held by each owner. The procedure adopted for doing this often foreshadowed the methods used in parliamentary enclosures. An umpire or umpires, known as 'commissioners', were appointed to oversee the process and to arbitrate in any disputes that might arise. Enclosures of this kind had been proceeding in the seventeenth century and continued during the eighteenth century but, it is believed, became less frequent after mid-century, giving way to enclosures carried out under private Acts of Parliament. Parishes enclosed earlier by agreement were known as 'old enclosed'. We do not have any reliable estimate for the total amount of land that was enclosed by agreement during the eighteenth century, and clearly it was limited by the need to reach a prior agreement among the owners, and was likely to be restricted, therefore, to parishes where the land was in relatively few hands.

Nevertheless, together with piecemeal enclosure described below, it seems probable that the total area affected was considerable.

Certainly, in some counties where investigations have been made, such as Hampshire and Sussex, more land was enclosed by these less formal methods than by the parliamentary procedure. In Sussex as much as two-thirds of the open fields was extinguished by non-parliamentary means in the course of the eighteenth and nineteenth centuries, either by the exchange and consolidation of strips to make larger holdings, or by occupiers obtaining control of a whole field or even all the fields in a parish. As a result, common rights were abandoned by agreement or because farmers no longer felt the need for them. This evidence, incidentally, runs counter to the view of Dr J.R. Wordie, who argues that there was very little non-parliamentary enclosure after 1760 because nearly all the land that could be enclosed by agreement had been so enclosed by that date.[4]

The second form of non-parliamentary enclosure was the 'piece-meal' kind. This was usually a slow, gradual process by which owners agreed among themselves to take small pieces of land, ranging in size from 1 acre, to 5, 10 or 20 acres or more, out of the open fields or commons for their own exclusive use. The private closes that were thus created were often situated on or near the boundaries of the parish, or alternatively in the village centre near the farmhouses, and were valued primarily as additional pasture and also for their convenience for dairying, for growing vegetables or producing specialised crops, such as potatoes, hops, seeds, liquorice or perhaps woad or madder. These closes had been accumulating over a long period, and consequently by the eighteenth century were known in open-field villages as the 'old enclosures'. They continued to grow during that century, and in some villages had become so numerous by the time of parliamentary enclosure as to cover as much as a half of the cultivated land.[5] More frequently it was a much smaller proportion, but even so one of the grounds for bringing on a full-scale enclosure was the desirability of abolishing or reorganising the old enclosures, which, by reason of the haphazard way in which they had accumulated, had become inconvenient and sources of disputes, especially where access to some closes could be gained only by going through those of other farmers.

4. J. Chapman and S. Seeliger, *Non-Parliamentary Enclosure: the Evidence from Southern England*, Working Paper 28, University of Portsmouth Department of Geography, 1993, pp. 14–15; 'Open Fields and their Disappearance in the Eighteenth and Nineteenth Centuries: the Evidence from Sussex', *Southern History*, 17, 1995, pp. 89–91, 96; J.R. Wordie, 'The Chronology of English Enclosure 1500–1914', *Economic History Review*, 2nd ser., XXXVI, 1983, pp. 487–8.

5. British Library, Egerton MS 3564; Nottingham University, Manvers Collection, Kingston Surveys.

Some of the agreements under which these small closes were created have survived, and it appears that the procedure was not particularly unusual or difficult so long as compensation was made to the other farmers for the loss of rights involved.[6] Where opposition was slight, where the farmers as a whole appreciated the value of the closes, and some of them, perhaps, expected to have additional closes of their own at some time in the future, 'old enclosures' accumulated in the parish. On the other hand, the fact that in many parishes the amount of land in old enclosures was still very small at the time of the parliamentary enclosure suggests that either the need to increase them was not strongly felt or the opposition of conservative members of the community was too strong.

Lastly, one should mention encroachments. These were parcels of common land or waste that were taken in, most frequently perhaps for a dwelling and a little accompanying pasture, without the express permission of the village community, or, in the case of the waste, the lord of the manor. Where the commons were adequate for the needs of the villagers, or the waste extensive and of little value, no objection might be raised to encroachments. Some were said to be sanctioned by custom. It was sometimes held, for example, that a right to squat on the waste or on the roadside was obtained if a cottage or 'hovel', as the contemporary term was, had been erected overnight and had smoke coming from its chimney by the morning.[7] Squatters, from outside the parish, or possibly the younger sons of the resident small farmers and cottagers, were attracted by opportunities for employment in a nearby town or a local rural craft, though in the later eighteenth century they were appearing also in purely agricultural parishes. Sometimes the squatters on the waste were charged a small rent, such as a shilling a year, by the lord of the manor, mainly as an acknowledgement of his continued control of the land that had been illegally occupied.[8]

It is an important consideration that these forms of non-parliamentary enclosure not only affected collectively a large area of land, but also over a long period served as forerunners of parliamentary enclosures, and indeed were often contemporary with them. Consequently, the *idea* of enclosure was one quite familiar to rural communities. Parliamentary enclosure did not, as seems sometimes

6. Michael Turner, *English Parliamentary Enclosure: its Historical Geography and Economic History*, Folkestone, 1980, pp. 138–41.

7. J.L. and Barbara Hammond, *The Village Labourer*, new edn, 1978, p. 5.

8. Nottingham University, Manvers Collection, Kingston Rentals.

to be assumed, come suddenly out of the blue, to alarm and frighten conservative owners and their tenants. Its basis, the creation of individually occupied units of land, was a concept which was already long known and well understood. By the later eighteenth century, when the parliamentary enclosure movement was mounting towards its peak, there must have been few farmers who had not seen, or at least heard of, enclosures of land taking place in one way or another, perhaps as near at hand as the next village; or, in the case of piecemeal enclosures, in their very own parish. This may help to explain why the opposition to parliamentary enclosure *among farmers*, as distinct from cottagers, was not more widespread than it was, and why the initiative to bring about an enclosure came sometimes from the farmers rather than the landlords.

The scale of parliamentary enclosure

The long-running and sometimes acrimonious controversy over the effects of parliamentary enclosure seems often to be conducted without regard to its actual scale. The effects of enclosure could not have been universally felt thoughout the countryside because enclosure itself was far from universal. Except in the Midlands, the great bulk of the country was already enclosed by the eighteenth century, and when parliamentary enclosure came there were some counties which, having few or no open fields left to enclose, saw only a handful of Acts, and those largely confined to commons and waste. It is true, of course, that the private enclosure Acts were very numerous: in England 5,265 of them, of which 3,094, 59 per cent, concerned some open-field land, according to Professor Michael Turner's figures. It has to be remembered, however, that not every Act made sweeping changes to the village holdings. Some Acts, indeed, were passed merely to confirm the legal validity of an enclosure that had already been carried out by agreement; others dealt with only a small remaining rump of open-field land which had survived piecemeal enclosure; and yet others were passed to rectify errors or omissions in preceding Acts and so enable an ongoing enclosure to be completed. Consequently it is the acreage enclosed, rather than the number of Acts, that is meaningful. There are in fact a number of problems in adding up the acreage figures given in the Acts or the Awards (which set out details of the new holdings allocated at the completion of an enclosure), and as a result there is inevitably a substantial margin of error in any total figure produced.[9] However, while not pretending to absolute accuracy, Turner gives the total acreage for England as 6,794,429, representing 20.9 per cent of the land area.[10]

Dr John Chapman, employing a different technique of analysing a 10 per cent sample of Awards, produces for England a rather higher figure of 7.25m. acres, and a further 1.17m. acres for Wales. The total of 8.42m. acres represents 24 per cent of the land area of England and Wales, with a very high proportion, three-fifths of the total, consisting of commons and waste.[11] There are a number of problems here, too, for the accuracy of the result depends on the accuracy of the sampling technique. However, although Chapman's figures are considerably higher than those of Turner, they are not so far apart as to throw doubt on the broad result, namely that some 7m. acres were enclosed by Act in England alone, representing about 23 per cent of the land area. It is important to notice that the percentages refer to the *total land area*. If it were possible to calculate a figure for the agricultural area alone, including commons and rough grazings but excluding urban areas, mountainous districts, and roads, lakes and rivers, then a higher figure would certainly appear. It is impossible to say with confidence what this would be, but perhaps it would be unlikely to raise the respective percentages to more than, say, 23 (Turner) or 26.5 (Chapman). A more relevant figure still would be the proportion affected of the then existing area of farmland (including commons), but this is impossible to estimate with any accuracy. It would certainly produce a considerably higher figure still. All we can conclude from these figures is that parliamentary enclosure affected a very significant proportion of the country's agricultural land, about a quarter, or probably rather more.

It should be noted that the figures produced by Turner (and by implication those of Chapman also) have been criticised by Wordie. Wordie argues from a consideration of the extent of non-parliamentary enclosure in the sixteenth and seventeenth centuries that at least 75 per cent of England and Monmouthshire had been enclosed by 1760, that is, well before parliamentary Acts became the predominant method of enclosing. He goes on to argue that less than 20 per cent of the area was enclosed by Act after 1760, and that Turner's figure should be reduced from 20.9 per cent to

9. John Chapman, 'Some Problems in the Interpretation of Enclosure Awards', *Agricultural History Review*, XXVI, 1987, pp. 109–12.

10. Turner, *Parliamentary Enclosure*, pp. 179, 181.

11. John Chapman, 'The Extent and Nature of Parliamentary Enclosure', *Agricultural History Review*, XXXV, 1987, p. 28.

less than 20.1 per cent. The major point he is making, however, is not so much the accuracy of Turner's figures as the extent and importance of enclosure that had occurred prior to 1760, principally in the course of the seventeenth century, and, in consequence, the somewhat diminished significance of parliamentary enclosure and the vast amount of historical discussion to which it has given rise.[12]

Whatever the true figure, we are considering a legal process which affected either as *much* as about a quarter of the land available for agricultural use, or as *little* as about a quarter of that area, depending on one's point of view. What is certain is that only a *minor*, if very substantial, part of the land was affected. However, the historical significance given to enclosure has always been influenced by the fact that in one part of the country, the Midlands, much more than a quarter was affected (see Maps 1 and 2, pp. 160–1). In terms of total area, Turner calculated that four counties – Cambridgeshire, Huntingdonshire, Northamptonshire and Oxfordshire – had more than 50 per cent of their area affected by parliamentary enclosure, including that under the General Acts of the nineteenth century as well as the private Acts of the eighteenth and early nineteenth centuries. Another four counties – Bedfordshire, Leicestershire, Rutland and the East Riding of Yorkshire – had between 40 and 50 per cent of their total area affected. And six further counties had between 30 and 40 per cent affected: Berkshire, Buckinghamshire, Lincolnshire, Norfolk, Nottinghamshire and Warwickshire. Altogether, fourteen counties, most of them in the Midlands, had over 30 per cent of the area affected by parliamentary enclosure. According to Turner's figures, the total acreage involved in these fourteen counties was about 3.54m., and this figure represented 52 per cent of the total English acreage affected by parliamentary enclosure.[13]

Before going further, it should be noted that there were three main types of enclosure Acts. The first and most important, both in terms of acreage and in historical controversy, was the enclosure of open fields and their associated commons by private Acts, each affecting only one parish or a small number of neighbouring parishes. Almost all of the open fields subject to parliamentary enclosure were enclosed by these private Acts. Secondly, there were numerous private Acts that were concerned only with commons and waste lands, Acts in which no open arable fields were included.

---

12. Wordie, 'Chronology of English Enclosure', pp. 486–7, 501.
13. Turner, *Parliamentary Enclosure*, pp. 178–81.

And thirdly, there were the commons and waste lands, and a very small area of open fields, that were enclosed under a series of General Enclosure Acts, beginning in 1836.

The figure of 3.54m. acres given above for the fourteen most heavily enclosed counties includes the commons and waste enclosed under both private and General Acts. However, in most of these counties there was little such land to be enclosed, apart from the commons which were included in the private Acts when the open-field arable was enclosed. But in a few counties, such as Lincolnshire and Norfolk, the commons and waste enclosed separately from the open fields did form a considerable proportion of the whole. For the fourteen counties taken together, the deduction of the separately enclosed commons and waste reduces the total affected from 3.54m. to 3.09m. acres. However, it was the open-field arable and their commons which has been at the centre of controversy, while the relatively small acreages affected by the General Enclosure Acts have earned little attention. In the fourteen heavily enclosed counties the open-field arable and associated commons enclosed by private Acts came to 2.95m. acres, or over 69 per cent of the whole of such land in England. [14] This high figure illustrates very clearly how greatly concentrated was this kind of enclosure in these fourteen counties, and why so much of the historical controversy has centred on them.

With this high concentration of open-field enclosure in a limited part of the country, it follows, of course, that large areas saw very little such enclosure, or indeed little enclosure of any kind. In the eleven least affected counties – those having less than 10 per cent of the county area affected – the percentage of land involved in any kind of parliamentary enclosure was on average only a little over 4 per cent. These counties were: Cheshire, Cornwall, Devon, Essex, the Isle of Wight, Herefordshire, Kent, Lancashire, Monmouthshire, Shropshire and Sussex. And in regard to open-field arable and associated commons enclosed by private Act alone, the figure was as low as 0.8 per cent, five of the counties (Cornwall, Devon, the Isle of Wight, Kent and Lancashire) having no land at all in this category. If a limit of under 20 per cent of the county area affected by open-field arable enclosed by private Acts is taken as appropriate for 'lightly involved' counties, then another sixteen would be added to the eleven above. These sixteen counties are: Cumberland, Derbyshire, Dorset, Durham, Hampshire, Hertfordshire, Middlesex,

14. Ibid., pp. 178–9.

Northumberland, Somerset, Staffordshire, Suffolk, Surrey, Westmorland, Worcestershire and the North and West Ridings of Yorkshire. The average proportion of the area affected of the whole twenty-seven counties remains very low, at 4.6 per cent.[15]

The reason for providing these figures is simply to reinforce the very important point that enclosure by private Act of open-field arable and associated commons – the type of enclosure, to repeat, which has been the subject of the greatest controversy – was very much a regional matter, affecting mainly the Midlands, and having a very small or even negligible impact in many counties in southern, western and northern England. Sixteen counties, only, had over 20 per cent of their total area affected by private Act enclosure of open-field arable and associated commons: Bedfordshire, Berkshire, Buckinghamshire, Cambridgeshire, Gloucestershire, Huntingdonshire, Leicestershire, Lincolnshire, Norfolk, Northamptonshire, Nottinghamshire, Oxfordshire, Rutland, Warwickshire, Wiltshire and the East Riding of Yorkshire. The average proportion of total area affected in these counties was 35.5 per cent. Averages, however, do not tell the whole story, for eight of these counties were severely affected, with a figure of over 40 per cent. In order of percentage affected they were: Northamptonshire (50) Huntingdonshire (46.6), Bedfordshire (43.5), Oxfordshire (43.0), Cambridgeshire (42.7), Leicestershire (42.6), Rutland (40.7) and the East Riding of Yorkshire (40.7).[16]

It was this belt of central English counties that had the greatest experience of private Act enclosure, together with the eight nearby counties that were less, but still heavily, affected. But in twenty-seven other counties of England the enclosure of open-field arable and associated commons was very slight. This geographical divergence is fundamental to an understanding of the subject of parliamentary enclosure. It did *not* have nation-wide effects. Indeed, over much of the country the effects were so slight as to be insignificant as possible causes of general rural poverty or unrest. On the other hand, where it was most experienced, in the eight 40 per cent-plus counties listed above, it caused changes that undoubtedly were widely felt by a large proportion of the country's rural inhabitants. Nevertheless, it is a striking fact that when the Swing riots broke out in 1830 the heavily enclosed Midlands remained almost entirely quiet, while it was in the southern and south-eastern counties, little affected by enclosure, that the riots were concentrated. Indeed, the modern historians of the Swing riots could cite only three of a total

15. Ibid., pp. 180–1.   16. Ibid.

of 1,475 incidents as being directly caused by enclosure.[17] Obviously, other factors were at work. We must be cautious, therefore, in ascribing to enclosure effects for which it could not have been responsible; equally, we must be cautious in accepting as influential everywhere those effects which can be ascribed to enclosure in the heavily enclosed counties.

Of course, if the private Act enclosures that were concerned solely with commons and waste are taken into account, the geographical area affected is considerably widened. There were counties like Cumberland, Durham, Northumberland, Somerset, Westmorland and the North Riding of Yorkshire where there was little open-field land to enclose but fairly substantial areas of waste worth the cost of taking into cultivation. However, adding this kind of enclosure to that of open-field arable does not alter the picture very greatly in the counties which had large acreages of open fields enclosed by Act. For the eight most heavily enclosed counties an average of only 2.5 per cent of the county area is added (although the figure is as high as 7.7 per cent in Cambridgeshire and 4.0 per cent in Leicestershire).[18] Moreover, it has to be remembered that enclosure of commons and waste had relatively limited effects in sparsely populated districts where such land was extensive, and that everywhere it represented an addition to the cultivated acreage, providing new arable land or additional grazing. As such, it generally had beneficial effects, adding to regular employment on farms and increasing supplies of food, and in the heavily enclosed Midland counties helping to offset any reductions in farm employment caused by the conversion after enclosure of former arable lands to pasture. (It was generally held by contemporaries that permanent pasture gave only about half the employment of the same acreage of arable.) In total, according to Turner's figures, 5.8 per cent of the area of England was affected by those private Acts which were concerned solely with commons and waste. The General Enclosure Acts of 1836 and after added to this figure, bringing it up to a total of 7.1 per cent.[19]

Chapman's figures from his sample of one in ten of the Awards give more emphasis to the enclosure of pasture. He found that in England the acreage of arable enclosed accounted for only just under 40 per cent of the whole, heavily concentrated in the Midlands. Outside the Midlands the enclosures were later in time,

17. E.J. Hobsbawm and George Rudé, *Captain Swing*, 1969, appendix 1.
18. Turner, *Parliamentary Enclosure*, pp. 180–1.   19. Ibid., p. 181.

were spread over a longer period than in the Midland enclosures and were more largely concerned with pasture.

In the Midlands, however, the proportion of arable enclosed was high: in the six counties, Buckinghamshire, Huntingdon, Leicestershire, Northampton, Rutland and Warwickshire, over 75 per cent. For the whole of England, enclosure of pasture – commons, meadow and waste – accounted for almost 60 per cent. Chapman's figures, therefore, go further towards emphasising the concentration of effects in the Midlands (where waste was scarce), and, by contrast, the relatively limited effects outside the Midlands: the regional character of the changes becomes even more marked. Outside the Midlands the much greater importance of pasture had generally beneficial effects, as mentioned above, and especially in creating additional employment. Even in the Midlands the far greater significance of arable land enclosure had its beneficial aspects, with more rational use of land resources, greater efficiency and higher production. The contrast between the estimates of Turner and those of Chapman thus has very considerable importance, though it remains a matter of uncertainty which are nearer the truth: both methods of estimation have their problems.[20]

The chronology of parliamentary enclosure

Two main aspects of the chronology of parliamentary enclosure have to be considered: first, the factors in its general rise and decline over a period of more than a century; and secondly, the considerations which influenced the timing of the enclosure of an individual parish.

It should be noticed that to plot the distribution of enclosure over time by the dates of the Acts is somewhat misleading. The date of the passing of a private enclosure Act by Parliament is not necessarily indicative of the beginning or ending of the process of achieving an enclosure. The bringing of the Bill to Parliament was not the start, but a stage marking the end of a preliminary period of negotiations between the parties involved, a period that might be relatively brief, occupying a year or two, or quite protracted, where there were serious difficulties in reaching agreement. Sometimes a proposal to bring a Bill had to be dropped because one or other of the major interests in the parish could not be brought to terms, with perhaps the scheme being revived at a later date when

20. Chapman, 'Extent and Nature of Parliamentary Enclosure', pp. 29–32.

there had been a change in circumstances. This might be the death of a large proprietor, perhaps, or that of the lord of the manor, succeeded by an heir of a more accommodating nature. Then the actual work of valuing, re-allocating and fencing the land after getting the Act could take a varying length of time. Generally speaking, the earlier enclosures, that is, those carried out before the 1790s, tended to be achieved fairly quickly, over one to three years. Later enclosures frequently took much longer, four to six or seven years not being uncommon, with some taking longer still. This was partly because the simpler, more straightforward enclosures tended to be tackled first, and the more complicated ones later; partly because the later enclosures were more likely to include provisions for the commutation of the tithes and schemes for road improvements in the parish, matters which could have the effect of considerably lengthening proceedings.

At all events, the date of a private Act is at best only a rough indication of the time-span covered by the whole process from initiation to completion. Nevertheless, on this basis the general pattern of the development of the enclosure movement is quite apparent. After some sporadic Acts in the 1730s and 1740s, the first large upsurge in interest in parliamentary enclosure began in the later 1750s and then died down in the 1780s; there followed, secondly, a great renewal of interest in the period of very high food prices during the Napoleonic Wars of 1793–1815; then lastly, after the Wars, the numbers of Acts dropped away again, partly because of the fall in prices, partly because by the 1830s there was not a great deal of land of value left to enclose.

Between the 1730s and 1754 the number of Acts averaged only a little over four a year.[21] It may be significant that this was a period when food prices were low, giving landowners little encouragement to go to the trouble and expense of seeking a private Act in order to enclose. Some non-parliamentary enclosures were proceeding, but we do not know whether this form of enclosure was in the doldrums at this time. And most of the few enclosure Bills that were coming to Parliament were concerned not with new initiatives but with the confirmation of enclosures already carried out by agreement.

This is an appropriate point at which to raise the question of why the initiators of enclosure should have begun to turn towards private Act procedure at this time, rather than continue with the old non-parliamentary methods. One object was that of achieving

21. Turner, *Parliamentary Enclosure*, p. 68.

greater legal certainty: the re-allocation of land among owners under an Act of Parliament was highly unlikely to be challenged once the work of the Commissioners was completed and their Award sealed and delivered. A second consideration was that under the authority of a private Act a number of objectives might be achieved at the same time, particularly commutation of the tithes and improvement of roads, though these additional matters were not commonly included until later in the century A third reason, and perhaps this was most often the predominant one, was that opposition to an enclosure, unless it affected more than about a quarter or a fifth, by value, of the land involved, could be over-ridden by the proprietors who owned the great bulk of the land in the parish.

Between 1755 and the later 1770s the numbers of Acts passed climbed rapidly, from twenty-two a year in 1755–64 to as many as sixty-four a year in the 1770s. This upsurge, interestingly, was against a background of a growing population and therefore an expanding market, and of rising food prices and higher rents for land. Then, in the 1780s, there was a temporary falling back to under twenty-four a year, partly because grain prices marked time in this decade, but also perhaps because of a rise in interest rates, which made the cost of borrowing to finance an enclosure more expensive. From the 1790s the upward trend was resumed, now against a background of poor harvests and extremely high food prices which marked the era of the Napoleonic Wars. Interest rates rose again, but the effect of this on the cost of financing increasingly more expensive enclosures was offset in real terms by the great rise in food prices, and indeed prices generally. Between 1790 and 1819 the number of Acts passed annually averaged nearly seventy-five a year. In the peak years of the Wars, 1800–14, when food prices were at their highest, over ninety-five Acts a year were passed. Then, after the Wars, as mentioned above, the numbers of Acts fell sharply, to only a little over forty-six a year in 1815–19, and to a mere sixteen between 1820 and 1844.[22]

Since the Acts varied considerably in the amount of land each involved, acreage figures are more meaningful. According to Turner's figures, before 1793 private Act enclosure affected 1.85m. acres of open-field arable and commons, and 709,000 acres of commons and waste. Over the war years, 1793–1815, nearly 2m. acres of open-field arable and commons were enclosed, and 905,000 acres of commons and waste. Between 1816 and 1829 only just under 240,000 acres of open-field arable and commons, and 143,000 acres

22. Ibid., p. 68.

of commons and waste, were brought into cultivation. In relation to these figures, Turner makes the point that his estimates indicate that at all periods the enclosure of land consisting of open-field arable and associated commons was the more important, but that over time the enclosure of commons and waste grew relatively in significance.[23] The enclosure of over 900,000 acres of commons and waste during the Wars is particularly notable when, despite rising imports, the country's supplies of food were failing to match market needs in the face of a rapidly rising population and a succession of very poor harvests, these factors combining to drive food prices to unheard of, indeed famine, levels. Some of the waste lands then enclosed proved to be too marginal, becoming unremunerative after the Wars when prices dropped sharply, and were subsequently abandoned. It should be noticed that Chapman, from his 10 per cent sample of the Awards, reaches a different conclusion from Turner regarding the importance of enclosure of waste in the later stage of the enclosure movement. He finds that 'from the start of the Napoleonic Wars onwards the waste was the principal target of enclosers'.[24] This contrasting finding is of considerable significance, especially when assessing the effects of enclosure, as we shall see in Chapter 7.

Whatever the importance of the waste in the war period, the great upsurge of enclosure which occurred at that time was clearly influenced by the extremely high prices and food shortages. Although the costs of bringing about an enclosure rose sharply at this time, and the cost of borrowing money also rose, it is likely that the promoters of enclosure believed there to be ample margin in the high farm profits and increased rents that could be gained. However, for costly enclosures undertaken near the end of the Wars, when the high prices receded after 1813, this may have proved a serious miscalculation.[25]

More difficult to explain is the first upsurge of enclosure by private Act, that which occurred between 1755 and 1780. (As noted above, the parliamentary enclosures of the 1730s and 1740s were mainly confirmatory of previous enclosures by agreement.) It is true that in the 1750s agricultural prices were beginning to rise after a lengthy period of depression for grain prices, but the upward

---

23. Ibid., p. 71.
24. Chapman, 'Extent and Nature of Parliamentary Enclosure', p. 34.
25. See a discussion of the causes of the large numbers of enclosures in the war period in Turner, *Parliamentary Enclosure*, pp. 102–34; and N.F.R. Crafts, 'Determinants of the Rate of Parliamentary Enclosure', *Explorations in Economic History*, XIV, 1977, pp. 227–49.

movement was for some time uncertain, while rents often did not begin to respond until as late as the 1770s or even the 1780s. Much evidence has been produced to show that in open-field villages the farmers were adapting their husbandry to allow for the growing of new fodder crops, and were also making other improvements.[26] But if the open fields were clearly capable of progress and higher production, why go in for the trouble and expense of parliamentary enclosure?

The answer may be that the open fields' capability for improvement was in practice often quite limited. The possibility of introducing more flexible rotations of arable crops depended on the nature of the soil, ill-drained clays, for instance, being unsuited to sainfoin or turnips; again, the soil determined how far it was possible to increase pasture resources by making grass leys in the fields. The existence of common rights over every farmer's land was often irksome and a source of disputes, and, as post-enclosure experience showed, farmers were willing to pay a much higher rent for land over which they alone had control, even when the farming itself remained quite unchanged. The scattered holdings in the fields, still often excessively small and numerous, formed another nuisance which progressive farmers were no longer happy to accept. But the great limitation of the old system was the rigid division between the arable – the open fields – and the pasture in meadows, commons and old closes. True, the growing of legumes and roots in the fields, where the soils allowed, increased fodder supplies and served in some degree as a substitute for additional pasture, while under favourable circumstances leys, or patches of temporary grass, could be laid down in the fields. Over a period, piecemeal enclosure, where it was going forward, could also add to availability of pasture, and extended rotations and subdivisions of the fields might be introduced to reduce the amount of land left in bare fallow. But the fundamental divisions of the land resources into arable and pasture remained; and on some clayland soils the best, and perhaps only worthwhile, advance was, where possible, to convert the fields to pasture, and perhaps make use of the former commons and any suitable waste for crops. But none of this could be done without a full-scale enclosure.

Turner has suggested that perhaps it was a shortage of land for pasture that lay at the root of the first upsurge of parliamentary enclosure. In particular, he points out that in the Midlands, where the unenclosed open fields were concentrated, there was a general lack of waste that could be used as pasture, thus creating pressure

---

26. Turner, *Parliamentary Enclosure*, pp. 101, 137, 137 n. 5.

to make more of the existing resources. This he exemplifies by citing agreements concerning the 'stinting' or regulating of the rights of pasture in the fields after harvest. The mounting pressure is shown by a tendency towards a gradual reduction in the size of the stints, that is, the numbers of animals, allowed.[27] If he is right, then it appears that after the early Acts had shown their usefulness, an increasingly acute problem of pasture shortage made the obtaining of Acts for this purpose more and more attractive. Through a parliamentary enclosure the balance of arable and pasture in the parish could be radically changed, and often quite quickly. And of course, where there was the reverse situation, where there were ample commons but there was inadequate and worn-out arable, this could be remedied too. Once Acts proved successful in remedying the problem, owners and farmers elsewhere, faced with similar difficulties, would be inclined to try the same solution. And so it spread. The gradual rise in prices, and eventually in farm rents, made the diffusion process even more far-reaching and influential.

There may, too, have been a further factor at work, for there is evidence to suggest that prices for beef and mutton had remained fairly steady during the first sixty years of the eighteenth century, before climbing substantially after 1762. The prices of dairy products, too, were generally favourable over the first half of the century. Wheat and barley prices, on the other hand, showed great fluctuations, and in the years between 1730 and 1756, particularly, had ruled much lower on average than either before 1730 or after 1756. The price of wheat at Cambridge averaged under 29s 6d a quarter in the worst period, the twenty-one years between 1730 and 1750, compared with 40s 4d for the twenty-one years preceding 1730, and 40s 9d for the twenty-one years following 1750. Barley fell precipitously in the early 1730s and fell even further in the 1740s, while oats also declined in the 1740s.[28] It appears, then, that a price margin in favour of meat production and dairying was established in the two decades after 1730, which may have reinforced the desire of farmers in open-field parishes to expand their resources of pasture and look to large-scale enclosure as the means of doing this.

Turner's suggestion may be strengthened also by looking at the stinting of commons. The same shortage of pasture land in

27. Ibid., pp. 108, 136, 142, 145, 149.
28. G.E. Mingay, 'Landownership and Agrarian Trends in the Eighteenth Century', unpublished Ph.D. thesis, University of Nottingham, 1958, pp. 29–30, figs 1, 2; Joan Thirsk, *The Agrarian History of England and Wales, V–II: 1640–1750*, Cambridge, 1985, pp. 845–6.

Midland open-field parishes that had led to stinting of the grazing in the fields was responsible also for the need to make the best of the common pastures. The village of Elston, near Newark in Nottinghamshire, was an example of a parish where overstocking of the common pasture had obliged the use of restrictive measures. In 1736 twenty-six farmers there signed an agreement to share the costs of bringing an indictment against those inhabitants who were occupying land in neighbouring parishes and bringing stock from outside the parish to graze on Elston common. A quarter-century later, in 1761, and again in 1768, further agreements were made regulating what beasts were to be allowed on the common. Sheep were to be excluded altogether since, it was complained, they were eating the common bare and tearing out the grass by the roots, while the practice of turning all the cattle on to the common on the first of May was to be abandoned as it was making the grass uneatable.[29] Elsewhere in Nottinghamshire farmers agreed to enclose parts of their open fields in order to remedy a shortage of pasture, as at Cotgrave in 1717–19, and at Eakring in 1744–6.[30] At Laxton, a parish which has retained remnants of its fields down to the present, the growth between 1691 and 1789 of piecemeal enclosure for additional pasture resulted in a fall in the proportion of land devoted to arable from 50 per cent to only 31 per cent.[31]

However, before leaving this topic, let us give examples of a different situation. The village of Flintham, lying only a few miles from Elston where the over-grazing of the common was so serious a problem, happened to be blessed with ample common pasture, extending to as much as 450 acres. The existence of this large acreage, with its 'sound and dry [soil], fit for marling and turniping', as it was described in 1759, was cited as a strong reason for enclosing, since the large farmers of Flintham could gain little advantage from it, 'being unstinted and allways over stock'd by the Cottagers'.[32] Again, at Trowle, near Bradford-on-Avon, where alternative pasture was plentiful, the freeholders had put forward a scheme 'of great advantage' to enclose the common, it 'being mostly very Rich land'.[33]

In any one parish the actual decision to enclose was brought on, or was delayed, by a variety of circumstances. These, as we have just

29. Notts. RO, DDA5/239–241, 333.

30. British Library, Egerton MSS 3622, ff. 202–4; University of Nottingham, Manvers Collection, Kingston Accounts and Surveys.

31. British Library, Egerton MSS 3564; University of Nottingham, Manvers Collection, Laxton Survey 1789.

32. Notts. RO, DDTN 4/9–11.   33. Lincs. RO, Monson SC XCIII.

seen, might revolve round an inadequacy of pasture, the poor quality of the arable, or a desire to exploit the rich soil of a common. The nature of the soil in the parish as a whole might also be a major consideration. It was widely recognised that a heavy clay soil, water-logged in winter and baked rock-hard in summer, and difficult and expensive to work, was not readily adaptable to new cropping systems or permanent pasture, and was generally unprofitable. For these reasons clayland parishes might be late in being enclosed, while ones having rich, adaptable loams offered attractions for early enclosure. Relief and communications, too, might be factors: exposure to cold winds and severe weather was an obvious disadvantage for tender crops and stock, while, on the other hand, good roads, or near access to a river, canal or seaport connecting with major markets, constituted a definite attraction. Parishes situated on or near main roads, for example, especially those leading to expanding markets like those in London or the Black Country, were likely to be enclosed early, other considerations being equal.[34]

But other considerations were by no means always equal. As mentioned above, disagreement among the large owners in the parish – over their respective rights to the land, the compensation to be made to the tithe-owner, or even some more trifling question such as the choice of lawyer to prepare the Bill, or of surveyor to map out and assess the holdings – might lead to a postponement, perhaps for a long period. Turner has emphasised the opposite situation, where the larger owners held only a minor part of the parish and there were many smaller freeholders, each owning up to, say, 150 or 200 acres, who collectively could block the proposal. He found that in numbers of parishes in Buckinghamshire they constituted a conservative force which was effective in delaying the onset of enclosure. Interestingly, by the time of the Napoleonic Wars they had changed their view, influenced no doubt by the high prices of that time, and they then encouraged the reform they had previously opposed.[35]

This again serves to bring out the role of the farmers in the matter. Enclosure was not always a question of a few great landlords deciding among themselves what they would do, regardless of the interests of the smaller owners in the parish. Of course, this was quite often the case. But there is also much evidence of the reverse

---

34. For a discussion of the relationship between enclosure and transport improvements, see H.G. Hunt, 'The Chronology of Parliamentary Enclosure in Leicestershire', *Economic History Review*, 2nd ser., X, 1957, pp. 271–2.

35. Turner, *Parliamentary Enclosure*, pp. 157–8.

position, when it was the smaller owners who held the whip hand, and who either blocked an enclosure or pushed it forward, as it suited their interests. Although the large owners might do much as they liked where, between them, they owned as much as three-quarters or more of the land by value – three-quarters being the minimum proportion, it was generally believed, that Parliament would accept to pass the Bill – it was also true that where the smaller owners between them owned about the same proportion and were in broad agreement, they were the deciding factor. And many of the farmers in open-field villages were in a sufficiently large way of business to be very conscious of markets and prices, and to judge the matter in terms of the profits that could be gained from this thoroughgoing reform of the farming system.

The lesser owners, understandably, might be worried that after enclosure the re-allocated holdings would be smaller or inferior in situation to the ones they had originally. The length of time taken to complete some of the later enclosures, as long as ten or twelve years in some cases, might also worry farmers who were elderly and feared they might not live to see the matter over, leaving a widow or young heir to face the upheaval and costs of moving to the new holding. Other farmers were concerned about having to take over land that had been neglected by the previous occupiers during the protracted period of the changeover.

On the other hand, these doubts were often over-ridden by appreciation of the compensating long-term advantages that enclosure conferred. Some farmers were so enthusiastic as to make the first moves towards the change. In Gloucestershire, for instance, it was a farmer who in 1735 suggested an enclosure to Lord Hardwicke's agent, 'the generality of the Nation being soe much Improv'd by Inclosures'.[36] In Lincolnshire, Sir Joseph Banks, the celebrated botanist, who owned estates there, received in 1796 a letter stating that his Kirkby tenants had signed a petition to Lord Fortescue asking for the open fields of Kirkby to be enclosed along with those of nearby Tattershall.[37] And at Bromley in Kent a preliminary enquiry found that nineteen freeholders, owning between them 2, 117 acres, were in favour of an enclosure, while fifteen others, owning 1, 246 acres, were opposed. But the 'ayes' and 'noes' fell into no definite pattern: some of the larger freeholders were thought to be against the enclosure, and some of the smaller ones for it.

36. Gloucs. RO, D214 E18.
37. Warren R. Dawson, ed., *The Banks Letters*, 1958, p. 652.

More generally, a sample of the documents recording the consents or opposition of owners to a substantial number of scattered Bills again shows no consistent pattern. Sometimes it was the small owners who opposed the Bill against the large owners who were for it; sometimes it was a mixture of small and large men on each side; and sometimes it was the large men who were against it, with the small ones supporting the Bill.[38]

General Enclosure Acts

The private Acts under which the great bulk of open fields, commons and waste were enclosed from the middle eighteenth century until after the Napoleonic Wars proved an effective means of bringing about agricultural reform, but in many cases a slow and expensive one. A substantial, if often minor, element in the total costs were the fees charged by lawyers for preparing the Bill and seeing it through Parliament, together with the fees of parliamentary officials, and the expenses of bringing witnesses to London to confirm the signatures on the consent document (the statement of each owner's share of the land and whether he was for or against the enclosure). There was consequently a demand from landowners and farmers for a General Act which would simplify the procedure, set out standard clauses for Bills, and generally cheapen the whole business of obtaining a private enclosure Act. It was hoped, too, that a General Act would make it easier to include the commutation of the tithes with the other provisions. A General Enclosure Bill was finally prepared by the old Board of Agriculture (founded in 1793), and after a number of false starts was enacted during the food crisis of 1801. It proved to be a dismal half-measure. The combined opposition of the Church, worried about its tithes, and the officials and lawyers, concerned about their fees, was sufficient to emasculate the Bill, and in the end the Act, as passed, did little to reduce the expense of enclosure or to clarify the procedure for tithe commutation. Separate private Acts were still required for each enclosure, though they were somewhat simplified and perhaps a little quicker to obtain.[39]

There was then a long gap of thirty-five years before a second General Act reached the statute book. The Act of 1836 was

38. See Chapter 4, p. 64.
39. Lord Ernle, *English Farming Past and Present*, 6th edn, 1961, pp. 251–2; Rosalind Mitchison, 'The Board of Agriculture (1793–1822)', *English Historical Review*, LXXIV, 1959, pp. 42–9.

concerned with the relatively small area of remaining open arable fields, and it laid down a lower figure for the proportion of proprietors that had to be in favour to ensure success. The Act empowered two-thirds of the owners of open-field rights, in number *and* value, to nominate Commissioners and proceed with the enclosure; or alternatively seven-eighths in number and value to enclose without resort to Commissioners.[40] Previously no definite figure had been laid down for the number that had to be in favour, though in the past it had been widely accepted that for a Bill to succeed a proportion of at least three-quarters or four-fifths of the owners, *by value alone*, had to be in favour. The reduction in the figure to two-thirds would have enabled the promoters of private Bills in the past to overcome opposition more easily, but it came too late in the day, when the great bulk of the open fields had already been enclosed; and, moreover, the provision that two-thirds in *number*, as well as in value, had to be in favour would probably have had the effect of negating the reduction in value.

A third General Act, that of 1840, was the counterpart of the 1836 one since it was concerned specifically with commons and waste. A fourth Act, the General Inclosure Act of 1845, was designed to assist in preserving commons as breathing spaces and for recreation. This Act, while retaining parliamentary control, substituted the Commissioners for the parliamentary committee as the local tribunal of enquiry. Subsequently the administration of the legislation was entrusted to the new Board of Agriculture instituted in 1889, the forerunner of the present Ministry of Agriculture, Food and Fisheries.[41]

The General Acts played only a relatively minor part in the history of parliamentary enclosure. Only 239,000 acres of open-field arable were enclosed under the Acts of 1836 and after, compared with the 4.25m. acres enclosed by private Acts, a proportion of less than 6 per cent. A much higher proportion of commons and waste were so enclosed, however: according to Professor Turner's figures, as much as 428,000 acres, compared with 1.88m. acres, a proportion of over 22 per cent.[42]

In total, about a quarter or rather more of England and Wales was affected by private and General Enclosure Acts. Most of this very considerable area was enclosed by private Act alone between

40. Ernle, *English Farming*, p. 252; Turner, *Parliamentary Enclosure*, p. 23.
41. Ernle, *English Farming*, p. 252.
42. Turner, *Parliamentary Enclosure*, pp. 178–9.

1750 and 1815, involving for the age a substantial investment of time and money. The landowners who put their resources into the work must have believed the results would be worthwhile. Indeed, they had a variety of desirable objectives in view, and it is to these that we turn in the next chapter.

CHAPTER THREE

The Objectives of Enclosure

It is a gross over-simplification to suppose that enclosures were concerned always, or solely, with the improvement of agriculture. True, often enough this was a prime objective, as comes out clearly in the correspondence over enclosure. When a gentleman who in 1763 had just inherited an estate at Holwell in Bedfordshire proposed an enclosure to the other principal proprietor there, he argued the advantage that 'our tenants could make ye most of their land (which they now cannot) . . .'.[1] At this period the growth of markets in London, major seaports and rising industrial centres, and the development of better transport facilities for reaching them, were also influencing agricultural improvement in general, and enclosure in particular. For example, it was about this same date that the surveyor of the Duke of Kingston's lands at Hanslope, near Stony Stratford in Buckinghamshire, on the old main road to London, reported that rents and tithes there would have to be reduced because the tenants had been adversely affected by 'the Improvements made at a greater distance from London, and the Turnpike roads opening a conveniency of the London markets . . .'.[2]

The growth of markets and advances in transport (which included river navigation, canals and coastal shipping, as well as turnpikes) also had their impact in more remote areas, in the hills and moors of northern England and Wales. Further reasons which gave weight to the advantages of enclosing the waste lands in such areas were the numerous encroachments made on them by neighbouring farmers, as well as by squatters, who were taking in land, sometimes with, but often without, the permission of the lord of the manor. Yet another consideration in unenclosed parishes

1. Beds. RO: PM 1721/31.   2. British Library, Egerton MSS 3569, f. 70.

32

generally was the growth of old enclosures, a jumble of parcels of land which had become so inconvenient as to need complete reorganisation, and in some instances required also the abolition of common rights in them in order to make them more advantageous to their owners.[3]

Apart from these and other agricultural purposes, enclosure was often necessary to allow the expansion of towns, and for empowering the lord of the manor to secure his right to extract minerals and building materials from the waste, and to prevent encroachers from forestalling him. Often an enclosure had both agricultural and non-agricultural objectives, and frequently, in later enclosures especially, important motives were to commute the tithes and improve the roads. In general, whatever the objectives, there was the expectation that the advantages would outweigh the costs, leaving the owners with more valuable land, perhaps twice or three times as valuable as in the unenclosed state, and in the case of waste land much more so. In considering the individual objectives of enclosure discussed below, it should be borne in mind, therefore, that any single enclosure might have several objectives in view, and that agricultural improvement, though most commonly cited and frequently very important, was not by any means the only motive.

The inadequacies of the open fields

It was common form in the preamble of an enclosure Bill to describe the defects of the open fields that were to be abolished. The Bill submitted to Parliament in 1782 for the enclosure of Kingston Deverill in Wiltshire begins as follows:

> The lands . . . lie intermixed, and dispersed, in small Parcels and most of them are inconveniently situated in respect to the Houses and inclosed Lands of the Owners and Proprietors thereof; and in their present Situation are incapable of any considerable Improvement; and it would be very advantageous to the several Persons interested therein . . . if the same were divided, and specific Shares thereof allotted to them in Severalty, in proportion to their respective Rights and Interests therein; but the same cannot be effected without the Aid and Authority of Parliament. . . .[4]

3. Beds. RO: PM 1722.   4. Wilts. RO: Longleat MSS Box 16.

As was noted in the previous chapter, the open fields and commons were subject to a variety of common rights, rights which varied considerably from district to district and from parish to parish. The rights, in fact, amounted to a body of customary law, laid down, amended and enforced as necessary by a committee or 'jury' of senior farmers; offenders could be presented to the manorial court (which still functioned in many places in the eighteenth century), and fined accordingly. This body of customary law, though of ancient origin, was by no means rigid or inflexible but could be adjusted and developed as circumstances changed: for example to meet a problem such as over-grazing of the commons, or to accommodate the introduction of a different or more complex rotation of crops.

The most important right in relation to the arable fields was that of grazing stock there after the crops had been harvested, a right which in the Midlands might be extended to the whole village community, but elsewhere was often strictly limited to those who occupied land in the fields or in other parts of the parish. A number of separate rights governed the various uses of the commons. Where the commons were extensive all members of the community might be allowed access for their beasts to graze, although detailed regulations were formulated to keep out 'foreign' beasts (that is, those belonging to people living outside the parish and occupying no land there), as also for the tethering of beasts on the grass paths and divisions within the fields while the crops were growing. Where the commons were small the right of depasturing beasts might be quite severely restricted, for example by limiting it solely to those inhabitants whose tenements were capable of enabling the beasts to be kept over winter. 'Stinted' or regulated commons also specified the numbers of different beasts to be allowed on the commons, and the dates between which they were allowed to graze. The numbers varied with the size of holding which a farmer occupied in the fields, so that a certain holding was said to have so many 'cow gates' or rights of access to the common attached to it. Cottagers who had no land in the fields, but had some grazing of their own, might also be allowed to use the commons for their stock; and in some instances old-established families who had no land of their own at all might still be allowed to use the common if no objection was brought against them.

The right of turbary – cutting turf from the commons for use as fuel or fertiliser, or for roofing – was often restricted to prevent excessive loss of turf, being confined perhaps to landholders, and refused to cottagers of less than thirty years' standing or those having less than an acre of land. Frequently only small areas of the commons were available for the exercise of the right of estover, the cutting of bracken and furze (for fuel or littering of stock), and similarly for the digging of building materials, such as stone, clay and sand.

In regard to the waste, encroachments might be permitted by the lord of the manor if a rent or fine were paid as an acknowledgement of his rights and the parish community did not object to any loss of rough grazing or other amenity. Encroachments, particularly by squatters, seem to have become fairly commonplace after the middle of the eighteenth century, and perhaps were not unwelcome where additional labour was needed on the farms or in local industries.

At some time or other the existing customs applicable to commonable land in a certain village might be ascertained and written down, as occurred in Kingston Deverill in the 1780s, the record there covering three large sheets.[5] Each of the village's various meadows and commons had its own rules: for instance, four-fifths of 'Rabbits Mead' was cropped from 12 April until 12 August and then became a common for horses for one week, was shut up between 19 August and 1 October, and was then a common for horses and cows until 29 November, and finally became grazing for sheep only from then until the following 12 April. A four-year cycle was followed for this common, and different rules applied in the third and fourth years of the cycle. The four open fields in the parish followed a rotation of wheat, barley, oats and fallow. The wheat field was in crop until about 12 August, when it became a general common until the following 22 November; from that date access was restricted to sheep owned by those persons who occupied land on the downs in the parish. On the following 12 April the field was shut up for the next crop. Ploughing in the barley field (the wheat field of the previous year) began therefore on 12 April and the field was shut up in crop until about 1 September. It then became a common until the following 12 April, when it was sown to oats. The oats had to be harvested by 1 September, when the field was used as a common until 22 November. From that date it could be grazed only by sheep until the following 12 April, when, as the fallow field, it became a general common until about 10 October, when it was sown to wheat, thus completing the four-course cycle.

5. Wilts. RO: Longleat MSS Box 16.

These few illustrations from the extensive rules governing the farming of Kingston Deverill make it clear that in many parishes there was considerable scope for disagreement on their application, and especially where individual farmers were inclined to take advantage of any uncertainty in meaning. Disputes were also likely to arise where there was innovation in the farming and the customary rules were amended. An example of this arose in a Berkshire parish in 1759 over the making of new 'roads' or access ways in the arable fields, a problem which led to the seeking of expert opinion on defining the terms on which such roads could be established and used. 'Mr Hinton's Maxims' laid down that a 'harvest road' could only lead homewards – 'every step must be homewards'; a headland (a space left for turning the plough teams) could be a harvest road, but only if it led homewards; there could be only one road to a furlong; and a newly made close (evidently a subject of dispute) could have no road from it to the highway 'because ye Highway itself, before it was widen'd was impassable'.[6] The question of access roads might be an important one because when open-field rotations came to include fodder crops in a parish where the holdings were much dispersed and remote from the homesteads, it was difficult or impossible to daily cart the fodder home to feed stock kept in yards or stalls without committing trespass on other farmers' lands.[7]

The extent of the limitations on farming and the general inconvenience caused by the dispersal of the holdings in the open fields varied with the degree of dispersal and the size of the individual strips or 'lands', as they might be called. Where strips had been exchanged and consolidated the nuisance was much reduced, teams and implements could be used more economically, and less time and effort were wasted in getting to and from remote holdings. But even so, there were still considerable areas of land within the fields that had to be set aside for access roads and boundaries, and many occasions for disputes over trespass, tethered stock getting loose, and the neglect of some farmers to destroy weeds and keep drains and ditches scoured and clean. From the landowner's point of view, the more scattered and smaller the strips the lower the rent he was able to obtain from the holding; and when such holdings became vacant he might find it difficult to obtain a new tenant from outside the existing farmers and cottagers in the parish. One advantage of enclosing such land was that a wider choice of

6. Berks. RO: D/EPb E8 Ledger D.
7. See Arthur Young, *Travels in France*, ed. C. Maxwell, Cambridge, 1950, pp. 292–3.

occupiers became available; and a further point, as a Bedfordshire owner argued in 1763, was that 'the tenants could then cross plow it, and by that means turn up fresh soil, but now they have so small a quantity together they are oblig'd to plow allways the same way'.[8]

An associated drawback of highly dispersed holdings was the amount of land reserved for divisions and access, often known as 'balks', which lay between the strips or lands. At Elton in the Vale of Belvoir in Nottinghamshire, for example, it was argued in 1798 as a point in favour of enclosing that there was a 'great Quantity of Balks (viz. one to every Land and some nearly as large as the Land itself, and very little is got from them except in the Fallow Year by keeping Sheep there for the support and management of the Land . . .)'. On the other hand, enclosure at Elton was made less attractive by the 'large Quantities of bad Land which will be very ill drained that the Improvem[t] will not be so great as on the first sight might be expected from its general appearance, and more particularly so as its heavy clay land in general which does not improve by inclosing equal to that of a lighter and gentler Soil'.[9]

It is questionable how far the dispersal of the holdings in the open fields restricted the farmers' choice of crops. Certainly the existence of such a limitation was often urged as a ground for enclosure. At Pertenhall in Bedfordshire, for example, an investigation made in 1796 prior to proposing an enclosure found that

> it is not at all unusual for any given 10 acres to belong to 10 distinct proprietors, and no one proprietor has 10 acres lying together, and consequently every occupier is obliged to sow the same grain and fallow his land at the same time as his neighbour, even though a different mode of cropping or cultivating might, and in many cases would be, very advantageous. . . . The Lands are well adapted for Clover, Rye grass, turnips, and some part for excellent pasture.[10]

By contrast, historians have gathered plenty of evidence to show that intermingled holdings need be no bar to the adoption of up-to-date rotations. Much depended on the nature of the soil and the attitudes and flexibility of the farmers.[11]

Another supposed disadvantage of open-field villages was the ease with which disease spread among livestock grazed in common. At Pertenhall in 1796 it was claimed that

8. Beds. RO: PM 1722.   9. British Library, Egerton MSS 3626, f. 166.
10. Beds. RO: DD WG 7/1.
11. See, for example, R.A.C. Parker, *Coke of Norfolk: a Financial and Agricultural Study, 1707–1842*, Oxford, 1975, pp. 85–6.

The farmers in the parish very often lose their Sheep in the open fields from the Rot, which never occurs in the old Inclosures in the parish. . . . This has happened several times within this few years, and it is one of the material reasons why the farmers do no good in the parish. . . . George Freer is a Farmer and rents about 152 acres. Can prove the losses by Rot in Sheep. . . .[12]

Liability to liver rot in sheep (a disease encouraged by badly drained pastures) was a complaint commonly made about open-field farming, while grazing in common was also likely to cause the spread of 'cattle plague' (rinderpest), which was a cause of serious losses of cattle in many years of the eighteenth century. However, it has to be remembered that veterinary knowledge was still very rudimentary, and that farmers suffered losses from these and other diseases in enclosed pastures as well as in open fields and commons. Farmers certainly recognised the relevance of ill-drained pastures to sheep rot, while the need to isolate and slaughter infected cattle was brought home by the government in its measures to control the cattle plague. Government intervention to control the cattle plague by compulsory slaughtering of diseased cattle, with compensation paid to the farmers and restrictions on cattle movements, proved very successful in stamping out the epidemic of 1714–15. It was less so, however, in the much more prolonged outbreak of 1745 which lasted down to 1758, while more limited and short-lived outbreaks in 1769 and 1774 were rapidly suppressed.[13]

Consequently, where farmers had better control over what pastures were used and could follow the government lead in taking steps to isolate diseased cattle, as on enclosed land, it seems likely that losses would be less heavy there than in open-field farms.

The old enclosures in open-field parishes, while useful for additional pasture and other purposes, were often not as advantageous to their occupiers as they might have been. Of course, those farms which included no old enclosures were considered less valuable and were lower rented; but the piecemeal development of old enclosures over a lengthy period had led to some of them being not only very small but also remote from the homestead or difficult of access. Often access to them could be gained only through other farmers' lands and closes, frequently leading to disputes and claims for damages. Thus a late eighteenth-century valuation of the Duke of Ancaster's Yorkshire estate of Haddesley observed that

12. Beds. RO: DD WG 7/1.
13. See R.J. Moore-Colyer, 'Livestock', in G.E. Mingay, ed., *The Agrarian History of England and Wales, VI: 1750–1850*, Cambridge, 1989, pp. 358–9.

The Old Inclosures at West Haddesley lye at such a distance from the Farm Houses and from each other that they are worth but little. Upon an Inclosure they might be laid together and adjoining the Field Lands. . . . The Old Inclosures lye strangely intermixed, some of the small Closes of One or Two Acres a Person must go through five or six others to come at them. Some of the small Tenants Closes lye half-a-mile apart. . . . Several of the small Closes might be laid into one, for at present the Hedges and Brambles take up one third of the Ground in these small Crofts.

Moreover, it appears that in some parishes the old enclosures had never been completely exempted from other farmers' rights of pasture. At Holwell in Bedfordshire in 1763 the tenants of old enclosures 'very justly' termed them 'half lands' (that is, half open)

because everybody has a right to turn stock into these fields in the same manner they do into the Common fields, which prevents our tenants from sowing turnips or Grass seeds in them, which would not only be a very great profit to them but greatly improve the Ground.'[14]

Lastly, there was perhaps some truth in the contention that open-field farmers were more conservative in their ideas than those whose land was enclosed. This view was expressed as early as 1653 by Walter Blith, and was widely repeated in the eighteenth century, particularly by Arthur Young. In a mainly open-field district lying between Cambridge and St Neots, Young viewed in 1791

for six or seven miles the worst husbandry I hope in Great Britain. . . . Bid the current of national improvement roll back three centuries and we may imagine a period of ignorance adequate to the exhibition of such exertions! . . . There seems somewhat of a coincidence between the state of cultivation within sight of the venerable spires of Cambridge and the utter neglect of agriculture in the establishments of that University.

Young was heavily biased against open fields and in favour of enclosures, although to be fair he did occasionally notice an enclosure where the farming had not improved:

At Knapwell there is a parliamentary enclosure, and such wretched husbandry in it that I cannot well understand for what they enclosed relative to management; rent is the only explanation, which has risen from 5s tithed to 10s or 11s free.'[15]

14. Lincs. RO: 2 Anc. 6/116; Beds. RO: PM 1722.
15. Walter Blith, *The English Improver Improved*, 1653, p. 73; Arthur Young, *Annals of Agriculture*, XVI, 1791, pp. 480–2.

Against this eye-witness but hostile view of the standards of open-field farming has to be set the large volume of countervailing evidence gathered by modern historians. In Lincolnshire, for example, Joan Thirsk found that even in the less easily diversified claylands the open-field farms exhibited a great deal of flexibility. Already in the sixteenth century old practices had been adjusted to meet changing needs: where pasture was insufficient, parts of the fields were laid down to grass, or temporary pastures ('leys') were introduced into the fields; where the problem was a shortage of arable, the best land was fallowed less frequently and made to carry more crops by more generous use of manures.[16] And we have already seen in the previous chapter that in the eighteenth century some open-field farmers were introducing new fodder crops and using more flexible rotations than in the past. In these ways open-field farming could meet in some degree the pressures imposed by an expanding population, and could also respond to market trends as prices moved at one time in favour of crops or at another in favour of livestock products.

Technically, there were undoubtedly many drawbacks to the old system: waste of land, waste of time and effort, and, most serious, the permanent division – not an entirely rigid division, it is true – between arable and pasture. There were, however, compensating advantages. Communal regulation and oversight had the effect of setting a floor to the standard of farming: inefficient or lazy farmers were obliged to comply with the customary regulations and expected standards. And cottagers and small farmers who were ambitious and enterprising could gradually climb up the farming ladder by renting cheaply additional lands in the fields, and thereby gain the right to graze more stock on the commons. Most important, the common grazing, the folding of sheep on the arable after the crop had been harvested, was, as Joan Thirsk remarks, 'a pillar of the farming system'. The farmers' sheep were all combined into one large flock which was systematically moved across the fields by the use of temporary hurdles, night after night, so that every part of each field received a thorough dunging.[17] Even the kinds of sheep used were specially conditioned to the purpose, sheep which dropped their manure at night when penned in the fields. Farmers of enclosed land lacked this advantage: their flocks were usually too small to manure thoroughly all their arable. On the light soils of west Norfolk where the flocks were particularly important, this was

16. Joan Thirsk, *English Peasant Farming*, 1957, pp. 99–100.
17. Joan Thirsk, ed., *The Agrarian History of England and Wales, IV: 1500–1640*, Cambridge, 1967, p. 188.

one of the reasons for favouring exceptionally large farms. Most farmers felt a need for external manures for their enclosed lands, for materials such as marl, chalk and lime, for 'town muck' (street sweepings, stable manure and 'night soil' from cesspools), ashes and soot, the waste of slaughterhouses, breweries and distilleries, seaweed, even old clothes and boots.

Much of the scorn shown towards open-field farmers arose from their being thought of as generally in a small way of business, ignorant and backward, and lacking in capital. In fact, however, there were numerous open-field farmers with holdings of between 100 and 300 acres, quite a respectable medium size of farm by contemporary standards. Early in the seventeenth century, as Joan Thirsk found, there were farmers of this kind in the Lincolnshire claylands.[18] Examination of Midland estate records for the eighteenth century confirms this situation, and shows also that open-field farms were tending to get larger.[19] Farms of 100 or 200 acres, and many of those below 100 acres, had necessarily to meet market trends and farm as efficiently as possible, for by the standards of the time they were considerable enterprises with substantial rents, wage bills and other outgoings to be paid. That they were able to survive and even expand within the constraints of the open-field system says much for its capacity for production and flexibility. On the other hand, it may well be that the unsatisfied needs of such farmers, in the face of mounting market demands, for the even greater flexibility of enclosed land lay behind the rise of parliamentary enclosure. Farmers' views on the desirability of enclosing were known to landlords and their agents, and reinforced the attraction to them of enclosing for gaining higher rents. And, in the long run, when population was expanding and prices rising, the open fields, whatever their scope for change, were seen as out-of-date, and their survival as imposing a brake on achieving higher output and more rapid agricultural progress.

Enclosure for minerals and urban expansion

The presence of minerals, especially coal, but also iron ore, lead and copper, and stone, slate and other building materials, was in some areas an important reason for enclosure in the age of industrial

18. Thirsk, *English Peasant Farming*, p. 98.
19. G.E. Mingay, 'The Size of Farms in the Eighteenth Century', *Economic History Review*, 2nd ser., XIV, 1962, pp. 469–88.

expansion after 1750. For centuries landlords had extracted minerals from lands on their estates, but generally on a very small scale. In the eighteenth century the growth of populous cities and expanding industrial areas, together with the transport facilities for serving these markets, greatly increased the demand for coal as a fuel, as well as for materials for building and a variety of minerals used in industrial processes. Landowners scoured their estates to locate accessible deposits, asserted their exclusive rights to exploit the waste, and ultimately resorted to enclosure as the best means of securing private access to the riches of the earth.

Particularly was this so in the regions of the Midlands and northern coalfields which became the centres of iron-making and engineering works, and fostered a host of other industries dependent on iron and steel for raw materials, on steam power, and on coal as a fuel in the manufacture of metal goods of all descriptions. A prime example of this process is the Dudley estate in the Black Country. Enclosures carried out on the Dudley property were little concerned with agricultural improvement, much more with establishing rights to the coal needed to fuel the Dudley ironworks, the basis of an industrial empire which grew to include its own private canals and railways. Formerly the minerals had been mined on a small scale by local occupiers, freeholders and copyholders. The object of Lord Dudley's enclosures was to bring this petty exploitation to an end and secure the minerals for his own exclusive use.[20]

Similarly, landowners in Cumberland developed local ports for the shipping of their coal, just as owners in other parts of northern England and South Wales encouraged the enterprise of new canal and railway companies, and invested large sums in the construction of harbours and docks. Some proprietors in the Pennines, Cleveland, north-west Yorkshire and elsewhere enclosed lands for the substantial revenues which lead-mining could produce. Even on purely agricultural estates where coal or lead were lacking, it might still be well worth while enclosing the waste for the purpose of quarrying building stone or for digging clay for making bricks, or quarrying slate for roofing, or sand and gravel. In many of these instances the object of agricultural improvement, if it were present at all, was a quite minor consideration.

Where large coal mines were developed, and perhaps ironworks too, it was often necessary to make use of part of the waste

20. T.J. Raybould, *The Economic Emergence of the Black Country*, Newton Abbot, 1973, pp. 70–5.

for providing access roads, wagon tramways, canals or, later, railways. Office buildings were needed for the use of managers and foremen, and also rows of cottages to house the workers and their families who were imported to operate the enterprise. Over the Midlands and northern England especially, established urban centres of trade and industry were expanding as well as new ones, and bricks and mortar over-ran adjacent fields, woods and meadows. Middle-class suburbs were created on the western side of towns, taking advantage of the prevailing winds to avoid the smoke and factory fumes, and working-class areas, together with factories, warehouses, shops and public houses, and eventually railway yards and sidings, in other parts of the town. From the later eighteenth century onwards a lot of green-field land was required to cope with the more rapid expansion of towns, some of them more than doubling in population in a matter of three decades. The Black Country town of Dudley, for instance, rose from a population of only 10,000 in 1801 to reach 23,000 in 1831, while the far larger Birmingham rose from 71,000 to 144,000; Salford climbed from 14,000 to 41,000, and its greater neighbour Manchester from 75,000 to 182,000. Of course, not all towns increased at this rate, and those which had no infusion of new industry grew only slowly, if at all. Nevertheless, owners of land bordering expanding towns were able to hold out for high prices; or, in some cases, by refusing to sell, prevented expansion and obliged urban populations to live in more congested conditions. Nottingham is an interesting example of an important industrial city whose expansion was severely limited in this way, hemmed in, as it was, by the Duke of Newcastle's hunting park to the west, the marshy nature of the land bordering the Trent to the south, and the small dairymen who held land to the east. This 'cow-ocracy', as they were called, found their business so profitable that they long resisted blandishments to sell. As a consequence Nottingham, from being once a pleasant market town, became one of the most congested of the industrial cities.

But generally the windfall profits to be made from fields and meadows sold for building sites were too tempting to resist, and where such land consisted of open fields or commons the promotion of an enclosure for the purpose was highly remunerative. Even some small country towns or middle-class spas, like Tewkesbury and Cheltenham, offered similar opportunities. Building development followed the Tewkesbury enclosure of 1811, while at Cheltenham an enclosure ten years earlier led to the appearance of a new suburb, Pittville, developed by Joseph Pitt, who was allotted land north of the High Street.

The making of capital gains from the conversion of agricultural land to urban uses was indeed one of the less common but still quite important and profitable objectives of enclosure. Greater flexibility of land use, whether for improved agricultural production, exploitation of minerals or conversion to building sites, was in fact the underlying basic objective of all enclosures.

Recent investigations have emphasised the wide variety of motives for bringing about an enclosure, and show that the influence of agricultural improvement, price levels and the rate of interest was frequently of minor effect, if present at all. In the Cannock Chase area bordering the Black Country, for instance, the motives of those involved were extremely varied. Lords of manors wanted to exploit their rights over the waste in order to mine coal or expand their estates, while the farmers of the district were concerned to protect their grazing rights and restrict the encroachments of squatters. The cottagers, too, wanted to prevent encroachments so that they could maintain grazing for their livestock and continue their access to wood and coal. The presence of expanding industries nearby created a demand for food production to feed the workforce, and to discourage workers' pressure for higher wages. Local industrialists also wished to expand supplies of coal and lime, and a particularly prominent figure, Matthew Boulton, the partner of James Watt in their steam-engine works, initiated the enclosure of nearby Needham Forest; he exhibited a hostile attitude towards squatters, holding them to be 'idle beggarly wretches', addicted to laziness and crime.[21]

Customary tenants, that is, occupiers whose rights to land were based on custom rather than law, played a key role in the enclosure of the Cumbrian commons. Again, the influence of agricultural improvement, prices and interest rates was small. Landowners in the district saw enclosure as a means of bringing to an end the customary use of the commons by small-scale subsistence occupiers, and were encouraged in this by the numerous wealthier farmers who saw scope for more profitable use of the land. Even small subsistence farmers were in favour because, owing to the decline of regulation by manorial courts, numerous disputes arose over access to common lands, while enclosure would result in enfranchisement,

21. David Brown, 'The Motives for Parliamentary Enclosure: the example of the Cannock Chase Area 1773–1887', *Midland History*, 19, 1994, pp. 105–27. See also N.F.R. Crafts, 'Determinants of the Rate of Parliamentary Enclosure', *Explorations in Economic History*, XIV, 1977, pp. 227–49; W.G. Hoskins, *The Making of the English Landscape*, 1955, pp. 279–89.

the conversion to legal certainty of their existing customary rights. For them enclosure was the means of improving their status while at the same time maintaining their livelihood as small-scale producers.[22]

Other objectives: tithes, roads, drainage

A great many private enclosure Acts included provisions for achieving a number of other valuable objectives: important among these were commutation of the tithes; improvement of parish roads; and improvement of drainage – in some instances the prime objective.

COMMUTATION OF TITHES

Originally, tithes were paid by the occupiers of land for the support of the Church, but since medieval times the right to receive tithe payments had, in part, been gradually transferred from the Church into lay hands. From the occupiers' point of view, however, it hardly mattered who was the tithe-owner: the payments, in any case, represented a tax on the yield of the soil. By the eighteenth century the manifold disadvantages of paying tithes in kind, that is, in farm produce, had frequently led to the substitution of money compositions, and where the tithe-owner was the landlord he simply added the amount of the tithe composition to the annual rents to be paid by his tenants. Both forms of payment, in kind or in cash, were a source of disputes and grievances. The farmers saw the tithes as a tax on their enterprise and efficiency, for the better their farming the more they had to pay in tithes.

The complaints, and the complications involved in assessing the value of tithes, increased in the later eighteenth century as markets grew and farmers introduced new crops and tried new ways of increasing their output. Payment of tithes in kind, where it continued, was regarded by the improving farmer as particularly pernicious, and was roundly condemned by Arthur Young. If payment were made in kind universally, he expostulated, it 'would be sufficient to damp all ideas of improvement. . . . I have never met with considerable improvements where the tithe was taken in kind. . . .' Fortunately, he went on, over a large part of the country a money composition per acre or per pound of rent was taken instead, while

22. C.E. Searle, 'Customary Tenants and the Enclosure of the Cumbrian Commons', *Northern History*, 29, 1993, pp. 136–53.

a considerable area had become tithe-free, 'which is every day increasing by all the new inclosures. The great objective at present of British agriculture, is to obtain a general exemption from tithe, by giving the clergy some settled income in lieu of it.'[23]

This was indeed a very important if secondary objective of many enclosure Acts: to exempt the occupiers from future tithe payments by making permanent compensation to the tithe-owner, preferably in the form of an allocation of land; or, as an inferior alternative, by establishing an annual corn rent, relating the amount of future tithe payments to recent grain prices, the payment being usually based on a seven-year average of the grain prices recorded in local markets (the tithes of grain were generally the most valuable). In the later eighteenth century and early years of the nineteenth century, when corn prices were rising strongly, tithe-owners tended to favour a corn rent. A third alternative, a fixed annual cash payment to the tithe-owner, was unusual, and became even rarer in the inflationary years of the later eighteenth century and Napoleonic War period.[24]

In practice it proved difficult to make an agreement with the tithe-owner that was acceptable to all parties, and so the tithes were not always commuted even where the promoters of the Bill had this as an objective. Tithe-owners tended to be cautious in giving up their rights, even when compensated by an allocation of land, the asset most highly regarded by conservative investors. Sometimes the tithe-owner strongly opposed an enclosure if it were likely to result in a conversion of arable land to grass since the tithes would then become less valuable, and in some instances he was able to block the project completely. It is uncertain what proportion of enclosure Acts did result in commutation in one form or another, and it may be that Professor Eric Evans' estimate of about 60 per cent is reasonably accurate.[25] The surviving instances of tithes paid in kind, whether for open fields or enclosed land, were left to be dealt with by the Tithe Commutation Act of 1836. However, it is clear that tithe-owners were aware of the strength of landowners' and occupiers' desire to secure the reform, and they were inclined to drive a hard bargain, sometimes an excessively hard bargain. Nevertheless, landowners were often prepared to accept even stiff demands, although where the compensation was made in land it necessarily

23. Arthur Young, *Political Arithmetic*, 1774, pp. 18–19.
24. Eric J. Evans, *The Contentious Tithe: the Tithe Problem and English Agriculture 1750–1850*, 1976, p. 95.
25. Ibid., pp. 95 n. 10, 96.

meant that owners gave up a considerable area, the sacrifice being regarded as worthwhile. 'I would with pleasure give up an hundred Acres to accomplish it', wrote one of Sir Joseph Banks's farmers in 1791.[26]

The bargaining power of the tithe-owner may be seen in the highly favourable terms he was often able to extract. Although the literal meaning of 'tithe' is a tax of one-tenth, the compensation made to secure tithe-free land was very much greater than this. In part, this was because tithe represented a tax on farm produce *when ready for market*, and compensation of only one-tenth of the land would include nothing to cover production costs; or, put another way, the rent received by the tithe-owner for his allotment would necessarily reflect the costs of production. Hence the tithe-owner claimed not one-tenth of the land but as much as one-ninth, one-eighth, or considerably more. By the 1790s it was common to give him so large a proportion as one-fifth of the arable land enclosed. The less profitable tithes of pasture lands were frequently commuted at one-eighth of the meadow land, and one-ninth of other pastures.[27] It was not unusual for the tithe-owner to receive altogether an allocation of from some 14 per cent to as much as 25 per cent or more of all the land enclosed in the parish.

Over and above the proportion of land transferred to the tithe-owner, his bargaining power is evident in the other terms associated with the transaction. The tithe-owner was exempted from paying any part of the expenses incurred in promoting and carrying out the enclosure; and even the cost of fencing his allotment was borne by the other proprietors. Similarly, where the tithes were commuted into a corn rent, the income from this was frequently exempted from future payment of local taxes, the poor rates especially, but also other local assessments, leaving only the land tax to be met. A further effect of commutation in the course of enclosure was that the reform did not always extend to the old enclosures, which remained, in Arthur Young's phrase, 'still to be harassed with tythes'.[28]

Incidentally, a consequence of the transfer of land was that where the tithe-owner was the parish vicar or rector he might well emerge as the largest landowner in the parish. This was one of the reasons why more clergymen were appointed to the Bench of Magistrates in the later eighteenth century as men of the cloth rose in wealth and status. There was nothing new in clergymen being farmers – they

26. Lincs. RO: Hill 22/1/8/2/1.   27. Evans, *Contentious Tithe*, pp. 97–9.
28. Arthur Young, *Annals of Agriculture*, XV, 1791, pp. 565–79.

had often cultivated their glebe lands before enclosure – though farming was not always considered an occupation compatible with the holding of a benefice. The Bishop of Salisbury's view was that 'the habits of life in which the clergy are educated, and the important office they fill are ill-suited to the occupation of a farmer'.[29] Nevertheless, many clergy did farm, and often farmed well, some of them being among the leading agricultural pioneers of the age. A large number, however, preferred to lease out their land to other farmers. When a clergyman received a big allocation of land at enclosure, not infrequently of the order of several hundred acres, he would most probably choose to rent it out, preferring to avoid the risks and trouble of farming and the expense of acquiring the stock and equipment needed for production on a substantial scale.

ROADS

An important objective of many enclosures was the improvement of the roads in the parish. The old lanes were often narrow, poorly made and badly maintained, deeply rutted and overgrown, and dangerous where there were steep hills and sharp bends to be negotiated. In wet weather, or after snow, the roads were often flooded and impassable, especially in clayland areas where the natural drainage was poor. In such districts heavy loads could be moved safely only in the summer months. Moreover, the passage of droves of cattle and sheep, and local movement of livestock, left the roads disgustingly noisome and unsavoury. In his travels Arthur Young frequently had reason to complain of conditions, even on the major roads. That leading from Billericay in Essex to Tilbury on the Thames, for example, he wrote in 1768, was so narrow 'that a mouse cannot pass by any carriage'; the ruts were of an 'incredible depth', and the trees meeting overhead prevented the sun from drying the surface; frequently the road was totally blocked by heavy wagons, which became so bogged down that each needed twenty or thirty horses to pull it out of the mire.[30]

Enclosure Acts frequently gave the Commissioners powers to stop up some old roads and build new ones which would be easier and safer to use. In 1781 Parliament (largely regulating existing practice) laid down that the roads built by enclosure Commissioners

29. Evans, *Contentious Tithe*, p. 79.
30. Arthur Young, *Southern Tour*, 1768, p. 72.

should be 40 feet in width (to allow easy passage of livestock); and also provided detailed regulations concerning the fencing of public roads and their repair and maintenance. The new roads had to be inspected by local Justices before they were accepted as satisfactory; and sometimes, indeed, the Justices ordered the Commissioners to recall the contractors to make good deficiencies. Road-making, then as now, was an expensive business, although the outlays involved in a particular parish depended on how many new roads were built and their length, and on how far the materials for construction had to be brought. Often the cost of making new roads was by far the single largest item in the total expenses of the enclosure. On the other hand, the new roads represented a major permanent improvement for the parish, and where linked up with similar new roads in neighbouring parishes, and ultimately with turnpikes and canals, greatly reduced the time and cost involved in sending livestock and produce to market, fetching stock home and moving them from field to field, and bringing in supplies of seed and fertilisers.

The advantages offered by Commissioners' new roads may readily be appreciated by a comparison of a post-enclosure map of a parish with a pre-enclosure one. For example, at Barton-upon-Humber in north Lincolnshire only two roads crossed the parish before enclosure, one in the north of the parish going from east to west, and the other from north to south through the middle, the old enclosures being clustered around the junction of the two roads. The enclosure resulted in an additional six roads, the Barrow road, Saxby road, Horkstow road, Ferriby road, and two roads leading to Thornton, thus allowing much greater access across the parish to neighbouring villages. A further three new roads within the parish were designed to give improved access to the holdings allotted by the Commissioners. The parish was now served by a network of well-planned, straight roads (see Maps 3 and 4, pp. 162–3). To take another Lincolnshire example: the village of Waltham, near Grimsby, had before its enclosure in 1769–71 only a single road traversing a small part of the parish from north to south-west and running through the two open fields there. The enclosure added four new roads, three of which were valuable for improving access to those parts of the parish not previously served by any through road.[31]

31. Rex C. Russell, *The Enclosure of Barton-upon-Humber 1793–1796*, Barton-upon-Humber, Lincs., 1968; *The Enclosure of Waltham 1769–1771*, Waltham, Lincs., 1972.

The maps of Barton-upon-Humber also illustrate some other interesting features of the changes brought about by enclosure. In this parish the old enclosures (shaded on the maps) were left intact, while the new allotments crossed the former field boundaries. The numerous new small-scale allotments were allocated near the village centre (as was usually requested by their owners), while the larger allotments were situated on or near the boundaries of the parish. Further, a number of the larger allotments, notably those of M.N. Graburn and William Graburn, were divided into a number of separate pieces, some placed at a considerable distance from the others. The same applies to some of the smaller allotments, such as those of James Bygott and Thomas Marris. Divided allotments resulted from the Commissioners' responsibility to allot land according to quality as well as acreage, and particularly so for the meadows; or in some cases this may have been done in response to the requests of the proprietors.

Obviously, some farmers were annoyed when the new roads, which cost them good money, skirted their farms at an inconvenient distance; or when some old lane, narrow and steep perhaps, but useful, was stopped up. Occasionally, indeed, they took their grievances to Quarter Sessions. But generally, like the commutation of tithes, the new roads were welcomed as one of the permanent advantages brought about by enclosure. Even today, more than two centuries later, the advantages are still felt. There are parts of the countryside where the Commissioners' roads have not only survived but continue to be superior to older country lanes. They run straight, with excellent visibility, and with a wide grass strip on each side of the carriageway, intended originally for the passage of livestock on the hoof. Unfortunately, where they make a turn it is generally at a sharp right angle – not a serious disadvantage in the age of horse-drawn vehicles, but inconvenient for the motor traffic of today.

DRAINAGE

Numbers of enclosure Acts included clauses giving the Commissioners powers to institute drainage schemes and flood prevention measures where farmland was liable to inundation from rivers or the sea, or where parts of the parish were too ill drained to bear good crops. In some instances, as in previous centuries, the Act was concerned with a large area of marsh, fen or moor, which might stretch over several parishes. Such enclosures were likely to be more

than usually productive of opposition, and even unrest, because of
the extent of the area involved, the large number of individuals
affected and, most important, the likely effects on the nature of the
local economy. Large areas of marsh and moorland were used for
a variety of purposes: for fishing and wildfowling, for cattle pastures, for digging peat, and for the practice of crafts using the
reeds, osiers and other produce of the area. Successful drainage
resulted in a very large change in land use, particularly the cultivation of crops instead of the old employments. Many people lost
their former livelihoods, such as they were, and had to change their
way of life or move away.

The Hammonds, in their classic study *The Village Labourer*, describe at length the events revolving round the enclosure of Otmoor,
a large stretch of common land lying to the north of Oxford. The
'coarse aquatic sward' of the moor was used as a pasture by the
inhabitants of neighbouring parishes, and numerous cottagers kept
their geese there. A first attempt to enclose Otmoor for the purpose of draining it and adding its 4,000 acres to neighbouring
farmland, was made in the 1770s and aroused intense local hostility. 'Mobs' of inhabitants prevented the notices of bringing the Bill
from being affixed to the church doors of the surrounding
parishes, but it was the dissent of certain landowners in only one
of the parishes that was really instrumental in bringing about the
withdrawal of the Bill. A second and successful attempt was delayed
until 1814, when again there was local opposition of a turbulent
kind. A petition from freeholders and cottagers was presented to
Parliament claiming that no lord of the manor had ever had absolute right to the soil of Otmoor, but this was disregarded. The costs
of draining the moor, said to be between £20,00 and £30,000 – a
very large sum at the period – were too heavy for many of the
cottagers to be able to pursue their claims to allotments, while Lord
Abingdon, lord of the manor of Beckley, one of the neighbouring
parishes, received compensation of one-sixteenth of the whole,
together with another one-eighth as composition for the tithes.

In the event, the drainage of Otmoor failed to achieve the
expected improvement in the quality of the soil, and the crops
were reported as 'barely sufficient to pay for labour and seed'.
Moreover, the Commissioners' drainage work had involved making
a new channel for the river Ray, which now tended to overflow
across a valuable tract of good farmland near Otmoor. In 1830 the
farmers of this tract, suffering severe losses, cut the channel so that
again the Ray inundated Otmoor and left their land unharmed.

The farmers were indicted for their action but were subsequently acquitted, and this success encouraged the former commoners to reassert their claims to untrammelled use of the moor. Five hundred protesters, men, women and children perambulated the bounds, destroying the Commissioners' fences as they went. Forty-four of them were taken prisoner by a troop of yeomanry called out to quell the rioting, but managed to escape while being taken to jail in Oxford when a crowd of people, in the city for St Giles's Fair, attacked the yeomanry. Feeling was so strong that, when later retaken, the prisoners, though found guilty, received very light sentences from the judge at the Assizes. Encouraged again, the villagers continued to pull down fences clandestinely, and the magistrates were obliged to appeal for troops to suppress the nocturnal activities of the outraged inhabitants.[32]

Another example of the over-riding of local opposition comes from the enclosure of King's Sedgmoor, an extensive watery waste lying to the east of Bridgwater in Somerset, and the site of the last battle fought on English soil in 1685. King's Sedgmoor stretched to some 18,000 acres, over which owners and occupiers in numerous surrounding parishes enjoyed rights of pasturing stock and of cutting turf, rushes and sedges. An Act of William III's time (10 & 11 Will. 3) had empowered the Justices to drain the moor, apparently without much effect; but its existence enabled opponents of the enclosure Bill brought in 1775 to argue that a new drainage measure was unnecessary. However, several lords of manors in neighbouring parishes stood to gain handsomely by an enclosure, and it was pushed forward despite a counter-petition signed by as many as 749 persons – only 213 persons had signed the petition for the Bill. In the event, the Bill was so much amended in Committee in order to meet the claims and objections of various lords of manors that when it was presented to the whole House of Commons it was thrown out on the ground that it was materially different from the Bill originally presented to owners in the country for their consent. George Selwyn, whose unhappy lot it was to report the Bill to the House, complained afterwards that efforts were not made by its supporters to muster sufficient votes, and that although opponents of the Bill admitted the merit of the enclosure, the difference in the two Bills was 'totally indigestible': it was a matter 'worse managed . . . than ever business was'.[33]

---

32. J.L. and Barbara Hammond, *The Village Labourer*, new edn, 1978, pp. 49–56.
33. Ibid., pp. 30–5.

The subsequent history of the enclosure of King's Sedgmoor is a protracted and complex story going on into the 1790s, a confused matter of continued local opposition, lack of clearly indentifiable parish boundaries, and the enormous number of claims which the Commissioners had to consider – 1,798 were allowed and 1,341 disallowed. As many as thirty-two parishes were involved, and the total expenses of draining 10,655 acres was £30,566, or £17 for each common right allowed – the Act adjudged every claim to be equal, regardless of the size of the estate or tenement that was claimed.[34]

Many enclosures, probably the great majority, left some villagers aggrieved, particularly over the loss of common rights which were niggardly compensated, or not compensated at all. Where the common was very large, as at Otmoor and King's Sedgmoor, and numerous local farmers, craftsmen and cottagers had enjoyed unrestricted access to an extensive area from time immemorial, the grievances were likely to be widely and acutely felt. The persons affected were encouraged by their very numbers to make their hostility open and evident, and this usually expressed itself, among other ways, in the destruction of the new fences, the symbol of suddenly making private what had always been public. Thus the enclosure of Haute Huntre Fen in Lincolnshire, affecting eleven parishes, gave rise to such prolonged destruction of fences that the Commissioners were obliged to go back to Parliament for new powers to make less easily damaged ditches in lieu of fences.

Unrest also occurred, however, in small-scale enclosures affecting single parishes. The Hammonds quote Maulden in Bedfordshire and Wilbarston in Nottinghamshire as instances where troops had to be used to suppress disturbances;[35] and a modern scholar, Dr J.M. Neeson, details numerous examples of open or clandestine hostility as well as non-violent opposition in Northamptonshire, including Wellingborough, Long Buckby, Brigstock, Rothersthorpe, Warksworth, West Haddon, Warmington, Duston, Denton, and other places.[36] This, however, takes us well beyond our present subject into the effects of enclosure on more general rights of property. Drainage schemes, such as those discussed, were particularly productive of violent opposition, and the more extensive the scheme the more widespread and long-lived was the hostility it created.

34. Wilts. RO: Longleat MSS Box 25.
35. Hammond and Hammond, *Village Labourer*, p. 42.
36. J.M. Neeson, *Commoners: Common Right, Enclosure and Social Change in England, 1700–1820*, Cambridge, 1993, pp. 263–79.

Generally, the more ambitious the objectives of the enclosure, the more likely it was to arouse opposition among both rich and poor. Major drainage schemes were perhaps the most likely to be troublesome because of the large area affected and the transformation of the inhabitants' way of life. But even where the objective was simply to improve the farming, the disappearance of the commons and waste, and the possible addition of a commutation of the tithes and road building, could cause major disruption to people's lives that was bound to be resented by many.

CHAPTER FOUR

The Process of Parliamentary Enclosure

Introduction

A relatively small part of the extensive literature on parliamentary enclosure has concerned itself with the detail of the process by which enclosure Acts were brought into being and put into execution. Yet a study of the process is well worth while since it throws valuable light on many of the issues concerned, and helps to bring about a deeper understanding of enclosure as a whole.

In particular, one is made to realise that the nature of the problems involved in enclosing and reallocating land varied from place to place; in some degree each enclosure possessed an element of uniqueness. Clearly, the physical character of the parish was highly relevant: the enclosure of land that was mainly open field and common obviously posed different problems from land that consisted mainly or entirely of waste.

But more than this, each parish, whether mainly open, or mainly or entirely waste, had its own peculiar set of propertied interests. The eighteenth century had great respect for property, especially landed property. The real asset of land was most highly prized by prudent investors because of its security and permanence (even if these advantages were less certain in those limited areas that were subject to flooding or erosion by the sea). In general, however, land had the great merit over other major investments, such as housing, government bonds, the shares of the Bank of England and those of overseas trading companies, that the risks involved were almost negligible. It was not very likely to suffer sudden unfavourable changes in value, although at times tenants might fall into arrears with their rents, or disappear with rents owing, or even have to be sold up as bankrupts. There were occasionally, too, legal disputes over title and boundaries. Nevertheless, land remained an asset which continues over the centuries, an asset that could be passed on to one's heirs and could also be used as security for borrowing, or to provide bargaining power when it came to marriage into other wealthy families. Moreover, when it was held in sufficient quantity it gave its owners local standing, social prestige and political power, to support, for example, the status of a county Justice or Member of Parliament.

Owners of landed property were naturally concerned about safeguarding it, and were cautious about entering into any scheme that might affect its value and its importance in securing local influence. However, land did not generally produce a high income: net of outgoings an average of only some 3 or 4 per cent of its value per annum, and consequently the major attraction to landowners of enclosure was its potential for raising the yield, perhaps as far as doubling the return or even trebling it. It is not surprising, therefore, that a major difficulty in bringing about an enclosure was the achieving of a balance of property interests, between large owners and small; between the lord of the manor, other major proprietors, small owners and owners of common rights; and between these and the owner of the tithes; and on occasions between a number of other individuals who because of some ancient rights or titles could lay some claim to consideration in the re-allocation of the land.

This is not to say that perfect fairness between rival interests was achieved or was even achievable. The very nature of a division of property and the making of compensation was bound to leave some owners feeling much less satisfied than others (as in present-day compulsory purchase in road-widening or new railway-building schemes). And in the eighteenth and early nineteenth centuries the deference customarily shown towards the greater owners must often have meant that, in general, their interests were likely to be better satisfied than those of smaller owners. When account is taken of the responsibility of the Commissioners to re-allocate land according to its *quality* as well as quantity and situation, the complexity of their task and the difficulty of achieving fairness may readily be appreciated.

Two other important aspects of the enclosure process will become evident in the course of this chapter. The first is that the clash of property interests was not always, or even very frequently, between large owners and small, but very often between the large owners themselves. In the numerous cases where more than one owner had a considerable stake in the parish, the bringing of the enclosure was often made problematic, and not infrequently delayed, because of the difficulty of agreeing mutually acceptable terms between the principal owners, including the owner of the tithes. And it was often not only the compensation in land that was the stumbling block but also what might appear to an outside observer much less important questions, though ones that affected personal status and pride, such as whose solicitor was to draw up the Bill, or the choice of Commissioners to carry out the enclosure.

The second point that becomes evident is the generally open character of the process. It is true that it was not entirely open, by any means. From surviving evidence we get to know only occasionally what private bargaining between rival interests preceded the decision to bring a Bill, or exactly what passed at the meeting of owners called to discuss the main terms of the Bill; nor when the Bill reached Parliament do we have in many cases more than a general impression of how thoroughly its terms were examined and what private pressures were brought to bear; and although the Commissioners' minute books and some working papers and correspondence have often survived, we can only guess at the nature of the deliberations which went on behind the closed doors of the inn rooms in which their meetings were held. However, a large part of the process was open and public: the meeting to discuss the Bill; the notices of bringing the Bill, which, by law, had to be affixed to the church door; the publication of the Bill itself, and subsequently of the Act; the notices issued by the Commissioners regarding the submission of claims, the display of the claims and of the surveyor's plan for public inspection; the display again of the re-allocation of holdings, when at length the Commissioners reached that stage, and any changes made to meet objections; and lastly, the public reading of the Award, in which the new allocations of land were duly specified and recorded.

It was, when all is considered, a remarkably public procedure, in which no-one could argue that he or she had been kept in ignorance of what was being done, and what was eventually decided. Objectors could petition Parliament against the Bill, though it is true that many such petitions were disregarded. The Commissioners, subsequently, were open to protest by aggrieved parties, and appeals against the Commissioners' decisions could in most cases be taken to Quarter Sessions or the Court of Chancery. Although no-one who has studied the subject would claim that the framing of the Act was free from private pressures, or that the results of re-allocation were entirely fair to all interests, large and small, nevertheless the process as a whole did offer some limited safeguards, and certainly a considerable degree of openness.

In at least accepting – if not adequately compensating – the claims of many cottagers and others to common rights, the parliamentary enclosures, as was argued many years ago, may be regarded as a landmark in the recognition of the rights of small men. Perhaps Sir Edward Gonner, in his classic study of nearly ninety years ago, was not too far out in stating that

> the Commissioners generally showed a desire to act with fairness . . . taking the conduct of the enclosures and the awards as a whole there seems to be no ground for alleging a general partiality on behalf of any particular class.[1]

Gonner appreciated of course, as have later scholars, that the *consequences* of the Commissioners' generally fair interpretation of the responsibilities laid on them by the Acts might well prove unfair to many people in the village, and even disastrous to some. A Parliament of landowners was naturally tender of landed property but it did take steps to regulate in some degree the process by which a large proportion of the country's land was reorganised for higher production. But all the consequences of that reorganisation were not foreseen, or if foreseen not found worthy of concern. The landed class, taken as a whole, and Parliament as its legislative body, failed to ensure that the essential modernisation of a large part of English agriculture did not leave in its wake a trail of dispossessed.

The Bill

The decision to go to Parliament to enclose a parish lay primarily with the principal proprietors, although as we have seen there is evidence that the original impulse may often have come from progressive farmers. If the parish were dominated by a single owner, progress from idea to the first practical steps might well be relatively simple and rapid, although it is interesting that Dr Chapman finds no relationship between single dominant owners and early enclosure; rather that this situation might be associated with delay. More important seems to be the presence in the parish of relatively

1. E.C.K. Gonner, *Common Land and Inclosure*, 1st edn, 1912, pp. 76–7. For an account of the open character of the procedure in a Norfolk enclosure see Naomi Riches, *The Agricultural Revolution in Norfolk*, 2nd edn, 1967, pp. 60–2.

large areas of open-field land; where this was the case the owners were more likely to proceed somewhat earlier than where the open fields were smaller.[2]

Where a number of major proprietors were involved, as was frequently the case, the first step in promoting an enclosure was of course to seek their opinions. It is clear from surviving correspondence that preliminary soundings and subsequent negotiations prior to drafting a Bill could be very protracted, lasting over several years. The main objections were usually those of cost, and whether the expected increase in rents would provide adequate recompense. At Holwell in Bedfordshire, for example, one of the owners approached in 1763 pointed out that the smallness of the parish and the fact that many of the owners were absentees, not residing in the parish, would make the expenses considerable (absentee owners were often not very interested in the matter because their land was small). Further, the land in Holwell was already rented 'pretty high', and it was doubtful whether it could be raised by so much as the suggested one-third. Moreover, materials needed for making fences and roads were very dear there. This last, however, was countered by the argument that quicksets for making live hedges grew well in Holwell and were cheap while, optimistically, 'a stone quarry may be found if looked for, and in some places a Ditch will do'.[3]

Correspondence of the years 1793–1802 between Thomas Davis, agent to the Marquess of Bath, and Davis's colleague, Nathaniel Barton, is also illuminating on the lengthy negotiations often needed to bring about an enclosure. The letters concern a proposal to enclose the village of Westbury, near Trowbridge in Wiltshire, and reveal widely divergent opinions among the owners. Some of them wished to wait for the passing of a General Enclosure Act (which did not occur until 1801), in the hope that this would reduce the expense and offer other advantages, while one owner was in favour of a division (presumably an amalgamation of holdings) but not an enclosure. There was support for commutation of the tithes: a Mr Smith, a farmer 'who is Dr Ludlow's factotum, will ride anywhere [to attend a meeting] to get rid of Tithes . . .'. Eventually, in February 1801, nearly eight years after Barton began his enquiries, agreement had so far developed that it was possible at last to call a meeting of proprietors with the objects of deciding what lands

2. J. Chapman, 'Structural Change in Eighteenth Century English Agriculture: The Effects of Enclosure', in H.J. Nitz, ed., *The Medieval and Early Modern Rural Landscape of Europe: the Impact of the Commercial Economy*, Göttingen, 1987, p. 143.
3. Beds. RO: PM 1721–2.

were to be enclosed, naming the Commissioners, defraying the expenses by a sale of part of the waste, and appointing a committee to prepare the Bill. Over a year later, in May 1802, Barton was reporting on alterations to the Bill that had been suggested by various owners, and on the progress he was making in obtaining the consents of owners to the Bill.

It should be explained that Parliament required the presentation of a document which listed all the proprietors in the parish, the value of the land owned by each, and whether each was for or against the Bill, or was 'neuter', together with their signatures. It was generally held that at least three-quarters of the land in the parish, by value, must be in favour for Parliament to consider the Bill, and preferably, for greater certainty, four-fifths or more. The figure was always calculated on the proportion of the land, *by value*, and not by the number of proprietors. Therefore, it was possible for one large owner who dominated the parish to have sufficient support by his land alone, even if a substantial number of small owners were opposed. In any case, the promoters of a Bill liked to secure as much support as possible. At length Barton was able to report that he had already nearly four-fifths of the value of the parish in favour of the Bill, and so it seemed likely to go ahead. But he ·admitted he had found the business of getting consents very trying:

> If you want to plague a man wish him to solicit an Inclosure Bill –
> I never knew what hope, fear, vexing and fretting were in reality till
> the last fortnight; I have not, as Mr T. Davis Jnr. lost an Eye, but
> nearly as bad, I have wore out my feet and spent my Money.[4]

In a much earlier proposal for an enclosure, one made in 1752 concerning Witham-on-the-Hill, a parish north of Stamford in Lincolnshire, the landlord was advised at an early stage to abandon the idea as the costs would be 'very great', and the return from the land to be enclosed inadequate to meet them. All his tenants were said to be 'much against it', and it would be 'very hurtful to 30 of y^r Honour's Farms'. The parson of the parish, however, a certain Wolsey Johnson, took the contrary view, arguing that an enclosure must benefit the tenants:

> and indeed how could it be otherwise when they want inclosure –
> when instead of having that parcel of land only part of two years
> out of three, they have it the whole year and every year to themselves

4. Wilts. RO: Longleat MSS 845.

– when instead of going a mile and a half to that land they will have it very near them – when instead of Tythe being taken in kind, I consent (in prejudice to myself and Family) to take a Tenth part in value of the Land, in lieu of all Tythes so far as the intended Inclosure goes, This, Sir, is no delusive way of arguing but an appeal to plain Facts, to the Common reason and experience of mankind, and has more or less prevailed in all the late as well as former Inclosures.[5]

It was clearly the fear of incurring high expenses that was almost always the weightiest argument against a proposed enclosure, while the advocates responded by pointing to considerations that would keep the expenses down. Thus in 1796 at Pertenhall in Bedfordshire it was argued the existence of old enclosures in the open fields, and of some old hedges and a brook, would make the work of division and subdivision less costly, while the making of a proposed turnpike road through the parish would mean that only short stretches of new Commissioners' roads would be necessary, and that gravel for road-making was available within the parish itself. It was true, they concluded, that there was no waste land to enclose in the parish, but that was also the case in a neighbouring parish and had not prevented the rents there from rising by as much as 10s per acre, from 8s to 18s, after enclosure, while more land had been brought into cultivation than before. In the end, the early opposition to the Pertenhall Bill was withdrawn only when a majority of owners supporting the Bill agreed to meet all the expenses of the opposing parties.[6]

When, despite doubts, arguments and counter-arguments, the matter proceeded as far as calling a public meeting to propose going ahead with a Bill, problems often still arose. Sometimes it was difficult to reach agreement on whether a solicitor should be entrusted with drawing up the Bill, and if so, who it should be, with one important owner favouring his own legal adviser, and another his. Thomas Davis, the agent of the Longleat estate, told another agent, Mr Bruges, in 1795 that he had never employed lawyers in any of the enclosures in which he had been involved,

> to save Expence as much as I can, and I trust I shall be able to get through this as cheap and as soon as any thing of the kind has been done. But as the well-framing of the Bill is the Ground work of the whole and as your knowledge of Business of the kind is so general, I trust you will come and assist me if you possibly can. . . . I will promise you a Dry Bed and think myself much obliged to you.[7]

5. Lincs. RO: 3 Anc. 7/1/15, 17.   6. Beds. RO: DD WG 7/1.
7. Wilts. RO: Longleat MSS 845, Box 23.

Similar differences, sometimes irreconcilable ones, arose over the number of Commissioners; and when that was settled, over who they should be; and similarly with the surveyor, who was entrusted with drawing a new plan of the parish. Unforeseen objections might be put forward at a late stage. A dispute might arise, for example, over who the lord of the manor, with rights to the waste, actually was, and there might well be more than one manor and more than one lord. Small proprietors might object that they had not been consulted in the discussions that had taken place over who should be the Commissioners and the solicitor for the Bill. Or some owners objected because their land was better managed and in good heart, while that of other owners had been 'Beggared out by Tenants who have failed thereon'.

At Kingston Deverill in Wiltshire, Lord Bath suddenly erected novel obstacles by saying that he considered the creation of small closes of three or four acres would 'entirely spoil the beauty of open Country', and would prevent his son 'for ever thinking of hunting there, any more than he would at Charing Cross'.[8] And at Waresley in Huntingdonshire the proposed commutation of the tithes attracted controversy, one advocate of commutation pointing out that, otherwise, a different system of husbandry adopted following the enclosure might result in the arable land being reduced, causing a fall in the value of the tithes; while General Needham, the owner of most of the parish, was unwilling to give up land for compensating the tithe-owner because the loss would interfere with his shooting territory.[9]

Examination of the records of a number of Cambridgeshire enclosures has yielded a variety of other examples. At Guilden Morden, for instance, the vicar objected to the proposed allotments intended to compensate him for the tithes as they would not be all in one place, and consequently he would have to deal with several different tenants.[10] Negotiations for the enclosure of Swaffham Prior occupied five years before the Act was obtained, in part because not all the proprietors felt they would be equally advantaged: one of them pointed out that since his land was already 'in good sized pieces' and 'in good heart' the enclosure would not benefit him as much as others whose farms were in very small pieces; in compensation he sought an assurance that on re-allocation his land would be

8. Beds. RO: W1/2169; Northants. RO: C (A) 3424; Wilts. RO: Longleat Box 16, letter of Richard Baker, 20 March 1782.
9. Cambridge Univ. Library: Doc. 664, 16, 23.
10. Cambridge Univ. Library: Doc. 637.

situated near his house. Another owner declined to sign the Bill as he thought the enclosure might result in lawsuits in which he, as a charity trustee, could not be involved.[11] At Shepreth there was a proposal to have only one Commissioner as a means of saving both time and money, but one of the owners objected to this on the ground that having 'some excellent land in the Parish' he would not 'feel easy at having my Land taken away and my Rights disposed of by one Commissioner'.[12] And lastly, at Litlington a Mr Dickenson was reported to be stirring up the farmers against the enclosure in order that he might continue undisturbed his illicit practice of grazing far more sheep than he was entitled to, as well as perpetrating other misdeeds in the open fields.[13]

Sometimes feelings became so inflamed over these issues that rivals printed and distributed virulent broadsheets entitled, for example, *A Caution against Imposition and Falsehood*, or, in response, *A Caution against Villainy*. Opponents charged each other with 'base and treacherous falsehoods' and 'impositions and insults'. However, supposing that such extreme hostility could be overcome and doubters won over to the proposals, the next stage was to have the chosen solicitor draw up the Bill, which was then read at another public meeting or circulated among the owners for their signatures. At the same time, to comply with Parliament's requirement, a notice announcing the intention of bringing the Bill was posted on the church door of the affected parish for three summer Sundays prior to the ensuing session of Parliament. A 'consent document', showing the names of all the proprietors and the value of the land each owned in the parish, was circulated. Each was required to sign under the heading 'Consent' or 'Dissent' or 'Neuter' (Neutral). This document, as we have noted, accompanied the Bill when presented to Parliament to show that a sufficient value of land was in favour of the enclosure.

Examination of these consent documents reveals that it was not always the large owners who supported the enclosure and the small ones who opposed it. Frequently the opposition consisted of one or two of the larger owners, or perhaps a small number of freeholders, while those favouring the enclosure might consist of a variety of owners, large, medium and small. At Kingston Deverill, for instance, the enclosure was supported by the major owner together with seven middling freeholders (owning between them 582.5 acres) as well as

11. Cambridge Univ. Library: Doc. 656, 2.
12. Cambridge Univ. Library: P139/28/6.
13. Cambridge Univ. Library: Litlington 1827–8.

seventeen copyholders who held rights to another 1,500 acres; only one proprietor, a freeholder of 131 acres, opposed the enclosure.[14]

A sample of ninety-two of the consent documents preserved in the House of Lords Record Office produced the following results. In twenty-six enclosures all the proprietors signed as being in favour, and there was no opposition; of these, ten concerned relatively small acreages, and one involved only two proprietors. In the sixty-six remaining documents nineteen recorded no opposition but a varying number of 'neuter' or indifferent owners. Taking the fifty-three cases in all where some owners signed as neuter, the value of the land so recorded was small, under 5 per cent of the total, in twenty-six of the cases; on the other hand, in fourteen of the cases the neuter owners held 10 per cent or more of the land, and in four cases as much as 20 per cent, which was the highest proportion found. Those who signed as neuter often included some substantial proprietors. Of the total of forty-seven documents which recorded some opposition, thirty-three showed the opponents to hold 5 per cent or less of the value of the land (also of the acreage, where this figure was shown). Seven of the remaining fourteen documents showed opposition of between 6 per cent and 9 per cent, and seven of between 10 and 20 per cent. The one case of the figure reaching 20 per cent must have been a marginal one for receiving parliamentary approval. Again, some middling owners, and occasionally large ones, were among those recording dissent; in one case it was the lord of the manor who was opposed. Lastly, it should be noted that in a small number of cases a few proprietors, almost always very small ones, had not given any signature – in one document recorded as refusing to sign but having no objection to the enclosure, in other instances as 'not to be found' or 'not to be met with'. Most of these, probably, were absentee owners who lived at a distance.[15]

It would be interesting to find if a larger sample of these documents produced similar results. In any event, one cannot tell, of course, what sort of promises or degree of pressure were used to persuade doubtful or recalcitrant owners to assent. No doubt, if they were important enough, they might be promised some kind of preferential treatment in the re-allocation of land. Where the parish was dominated by one large owner it is possible that the smaller men might assent out of deference, or because it might be

14. Wilts. RO: Longleat Box 16.
15. House of Lords RO: Proceedings at Committees on Private Bills.

unwise to offend someone who commanded local influence. Where the ownership was more mixed this might be much less likely. Certainly, estate records of the period do not indicate that farmers were easily cowed by wealth or rank; rather that they were inclined to assert their independence and react in a hostile way to undue pressure applied by a big landlord. And of course the figures above may be interpreted to suggest an alternative view, that is, in as much as half of the sample some opposition was recorded (though for the most part on a very small scale); and that in over 70 per cent of the sample some owners, sometimes holding a substantial share of the land, recorded either opposition or indifference.

One must assume that a matter affecting people's land, often their only valuable asset, and, moreover, an asset that had been inherited and was intended for passing on to heirs, must have been of very great concern. It is perhaps surprising, therefore, that the opposition was not greater, especially among those of a conservative cast of mind; and also surprising that so many owners chose to be neutral in so important a matter. Perhaps they believed that opposition would be fruitless, and knew of neighbouring parishes where this had proved to be the case. On the other hand, many owners must have been swayed by the advantages of enclosed land over that subject to common rights, and not least, perhaps, by the prospect of a considerable rise in its value when enclosed.

When the Bill reached Parliament it was referred to a committee, usually a large committee, for detailed consideration. Historians have produced a great deal of evidence that such committees could be, and often were, packed with the Bill's supporters; and that opposition, if in the form of a counter-petition signed only by minor owners, was likely to be set aside.[16] This was most probably the case where some important owner was involved. It was less probable, however, where the landowners promoting the enclosure were not leading county figures and commanded no particular influence in Parliament. It has to be remembered also that a significant proportion of Bills affected only small acreages or land of limited value, such as a poor common or a surviving remnant of open field left after a long period of piecemeal enclosure; and, furthermore, that some Bills were merely obtained to give legal confirmation to existing claims of ownership or to an enclosure already achieved by agreement.

16. J.L. and Barbara Hammond, *The Village Labourer*, new edn, 1978, pp. 15–27; J.M. Martin, 'Members of Parliament and Enclosure: a Reconsideration', *Agricultural History Review*, XXVII, 1979, pp. 101–9.

It is clear from surviving correspondence that when there was significant opposition the passage of the Bill could by no means be regarded as a certainty. Doubts arose, for example, as to whether the proportion of land in favour of the Bill was sufficient, particularly if it was barely 80 per cent. Again, any unusual clauses in the Bill, an unduly high level of compensation for the tithe-owner, for instance, or for the lord of the manor, might cause it to be amended or rejected. Occasionally the existence of a large number of very small owners might raise doubts as to whether they possessed sufficient land to be able to provide their share of the compensation for the tithes.

The correspondence of the solicitor for the Pertenhall (Beds.) enclosure of 1796, a certain George Bramwell, illustrates a number of these points. Since the consents to the Bill totalled only a little over four-fifths of the value of the land involved, Bramwell urged employment of greater persuasion to obtain more consents: 'do use a litle intrigue to get over some of the most indifferent of the Dissents . . .'. He warned also that 'a very accurate state of the property' was essential, as well as the means of proving it, since he had heard that a Mr Pagett, who opposed the Bill, had ordered a survey of his own to be made. A further weakness was that some owners of the old enclosures there did not have sufficient land to make compensation for the tithes, and consequently they would have to be got to agree to a corn rent in lieu of giving up land. To obtain support in Parliament he suggested that letters advocating the enclosure should be sent to possible opponents, as well as to friends and constitutents of the Members for neighbouring counties. It was important, he urged, 'to *see* and *speak* to as many Members as possible' and to inform them of the date of the second reading and secure their attendance. As for the opposition to the Bill in the parish, a petition had been signed by ten persons but only three of these had land that was affected by the enclosure, one an owner of about 100 acres, another of about 30 acres, and one holding a cottage right to the common. This last, however, rented the tithes 'at a good bargain', and it was because he would lose this lucrative arrangement that he opposed the Bill. The opposition of the owner of 30 acres, he noted, arose because part of his land had already been enclosed without authority (in return for which he provided a bull and a boar for the use of the parish); and as it had increased in value he feared that it would be included in the new holdings allotted in the enclosure, to his loss.[17]

<hr>

17. Beds. RO: DD WG7/1.

Professor Turner notes that the enclosure of Monks Risborough (Bucks.) in 1820 came only after a 'very bitter struggle' between the leading proprietors and the poor of the parish. A counter-petition was successful to the extent that the Bill was amended to allow the appointment of a special Commissioner for the poor. This Commissioner was a person of status – Sir John Dashwood King – and although he was dismissed by proponents of the Bill as 'a blundering blockhead' who would 'not trouble himself about the matter', he proved this a mistaken judgment and justified his appointment by contesting the allotment proposed for the poor with the other Commissioners. A difficulty that had to be overcome before the Princes Risborough Bill was passed arose over the question of the owners' ability to meet the costs. The counter-petition stated that the small owners there had already mortgaged their properties to a considerable extent, and would have to sell up and become day-labourers if they had to meet the expenses of the enclosure. This problem was met by a provision for the expenses to be met by sales of land.[18]

Dr Neeson's researches in Northamptonshire, a very heavily enclosed county, have brought to light many instances of opposition to Bills. Before a Bill was even drafted tenants were obstructive in neglecting to mark out their lands for the purpose of the survey, while the numerous persons who feared the loss of the commons included various tradesmen and craftsmen as well as farmer-artisans and cottagers. Some of the counter-petitions were brought by local gentry concerned that enclosure might result in increased numbers of poor, and hence heavier poor rates. In some instances opposition to Bills extended to as much as 28 per cent of the field land and commons, which did not, however, prevent the Bills from being passed. The threat of counter-petition, nevertheless, was successful in achieving the withdrawal of as high a proportion as 22 per cent of the Bills presented between 1750 and 1815. And when opposition in Parliament proved fruitless this was not the end of the matter, for in the larger villages, especially, disgruntled opponents vented their frustration by pulling down and burning fences, and by damaging the property of those promoting enclosure. Altogether, petitions were brought against 11 per cent of Northamptonshire Bills, and two-thirds of them had at least one owner refusing his consent.[19]

18. Michael E. Turner, 'The Cost of Parliamentary Enclosure in Buckinghamshire', *Agricultural History Review*, XXI, 1973, pp. 37–8.
19. J.M. Neeson, 'The Opponents of Enclosure in Eighteenth Century Northamptonshire', *Past and Present*, 105, 1984, pp. 118–21, 123, 125, 127, 129–32, 134, 136.

Taken as a whole, the parliamentary scrutiny of enclosure Bills, and the opposition expressed in counter-petitions, though often unsuccessful, resulted in a surprisingly high proportion of Bills being withdrawn – 22 per cent between 1750 and 1815 in Northampton-shire, as we have just seen. The figure is the more remarkable when the care with which the Bill was usually prepared is taken into account, and consideration is given to the often lengthy period of negotiation and discussion which had preceded the bringing of Bills. An examination of all enclosure Bills presented to Parliament between 1715 and 1774 showed that the proportion failing in that period was 14 per cent, and that over eight hundred Bills were passed into Acts without any counter-petition being presented. Of seventy-two Bills that were opposed by counter-petition, as many as twenty-two – 30 per cent – failed.[20]

That parliamentary scrutiny was not a mere formality is shown by the amendments frequently made to Bills to buy off opposition and ensure acceptance – amendments that were often of a significant and detailed character. When by the early 1770s the numbers of Bills entering Parliament rose to very considerable figures (263 Acts were passed between 1765 and 1769, and 319 Acts between 1770 and 1774) Parliament took steps to control the procedure better. An Act of 1773 empowered three-quarters of the occupiers, in number and value, to regulate open fields and commons, with any dissenting cottagers being allotted part of the common for their sole use. This measure, presumably, was intended to encour-age enclosure by agreement, rather than by Act. In the following year a number of orders were made concerning enclosure Bills. Notice of bringing a Bill was to be posted on the church door on three Sundays in the summer preceding the session of Parliament; the Commissioners were to be named in the Bill, and required to account for all monies raised towards meeting the costs; and in 1781 specifications for the making of public roads, and for their repair and maintenance, were laid down.[21]

Taking the much longer period of 1730 to 1839, it has recently been ascertained that of 5,494 English enclosure Bills presented to Parliament, as many as 1,453 (26 per cent) failed or were with-drawn for one reason or another. In nearly 40 per cent of the lost Bills a counter-petition was presented. The heavily enclosed county of Northamptonshire produced a figure of 21 per cent of Bills

20. Sheila Lambert, *Bills and Acts: Legislative Procedure in Eighteenth Century England*, Cambridge, 1971, p. 133.
21. Ibid., pp. 134, 141–3.

dropped, with 11 per cent of all the Bills resulting in the presentation of a counter-petition; the rather less heavily enclosed county of Buckinghamshire had figures of 22 per cent and 13 per cent respectively.[22] These figures point to two general conclusions: first, that opposition to parliamentary enclosure was by no means infrequent, particularly when account is taken of the numbers of enclosures unlikely to attract opposition, such as those concerning small acreages or merely confirming an enclosure already carried out by agreement; and secondly, that opposition was not a hopeless cause but played a significant part in the failure of a large proportion of Bills.

Executing the Act

Once the Bill had become a private Act of Parliament its execution was in the hands of the Commissioners named in it. These, normally three in number, were chosen by the proprietors. Frequently one Commissioner represented the lord of the manor (whose interest was mainly in rights to the waste, apart from any other land he owned in the parish); a second represented the tithe-owner in those Acts where the tithes were to be commuted, or alternatively a major owner; and the third the remaining owners collectively. There was rarely a Commissioner to represent the poor, although, as we have seen, such a Commissioner was appointed exceptionally in the Monks Risborough enclosure. Should a Commissioner resign or be otherwise unable to act, the interest which he represented had the right to nominate his successor.

To avoid unnecessary delays caused by the absence of a Commissioner, there was frequently a clause allowing any two to act. The fees allowed Commissioners gradually rose from a guinea a day in the early years of parliamentary enclosure (including days spent in travelling), to two guineas, and eventually, after about 1800, to three guineas (a rise explained partly by the effects of inflation, and partly by the complexity of many later enclosures). Sometimes the fee included expenses, sometimes expenses were chargeable in addition. As the costs of enclosure tended to rise, so the fees and the expenses tended to become more circumscribed. The 1813 Act

22. M. Turner and T. Wray, 'A Survey of Sources for Parliamentary Enclosure: the *House of Commons Journal* and Commissioners' Working Papers', *Archives*, XIV, 1991, pp. 257–88.

for the Elvethan (Hants.) enclosure allowed the Commissioners three guineas a day with expenses limited to the cost of their room for the meetings and a fire and candle; and three guineas a day for their Clerk. A very late enclosure, that of Marsh Gibbon (Bucks.) of 1841, specified for its single Commissioner a fee of three guineas a day, including expenses, for the first three years only, and two guineas a day subsequently; a 'day' was to be one of eight hours between 25 March and 29 September, and of six hours in the remaining autumn and winter period – for fewer hours only a half-day was allowed.[23]

What sort of men were the Commissioners? It has to be remembered that, except where the Act concerned only a small acreage, executing the enclosure was a major responsibility calling for men of standing and probity, men who could be relied on to balance competing claims, adjudicate in disputes, and produce a final result that was as close as possible to satisfying the majority of the owners. In these respects they were comparable to expert consultants like those employed in major construction projects of the present day. In addition, the Commissioners needed to have an understanding of land tenure and farming – they had to direct the farming while the enclosure was in progress – and also to have some knowledge of the law relating to land, tithes and related matters. The work could be complicated and exacting, and it is not surprising that on occasion the promoters were at a loss to find suitable persons to act. It was in this quandary that Professor John Simmonds of Bury St Edmunds wrote in 1801 to his friend, Arthur Young, regarding the Fakenham enclosure:

> I thought of old Roper for a commissioner, as he is a very respectable man, and lives not at a great distance from Fakenham; but I do not find he has had much to do in these things. The Duke [of Grafton] says it is usual for the Impropriator to have a Parson; but Mr Lord of Whelnetham is no more; and the bulk of our Parsons understand no more of agriculture than of Theology. Do you know a proper One . . . ? I have in view for a commissioner Sir William Beauchamp's steward, whom you mentioned, or Mr Cooke, a capital farmer near Hadley, who holds a considerable estate under Benet' College. He is an intimate friend of my tenant Stutton, who brought him a year or two ago to see my house, and I was much pleased with him.[24]

23. Hants. RO: 50M 63 Box 1; Bodl. Library: Dep. C 131.
24. Letter: John Simmonds to Arthur Young, 10 Oct. 1801, British Library, Add. MSS 35128, f. 380.

Because it was clearly advantageous to employ men who had experience in the business, and had achieved a reputation for getting the work done fairly and efficiently, it was commonly the case that permutations of a small number of experienced Commissioners were used in a large number of local enclosures. When the Bishop of St David's objected to clauses dealing with the tithes in the Kingston Deverill Bill, he was told that he need have no fears as 'the Commissioners are well known in the Country having been many Times invested with similar Powers and executed them to the satisfaction of all parties'.[25] However, such confidence could not always be guaranteed, and in Wales, where landlords were anxious to obtain legal confirmation of their titles to lands only loosely held, as well as to establish rights to minerals, Professor David Jones describes some of the Commissioners as 'men of dubious character'.[26]

For reasons of economy it was unusual in the eighteenth century to have more than three Commissioners, and occasionally only two, or even a single one, were appointed. After 1801, however, when the costs of enclosing were rising sharply, it became more usual to appoint only a single Commissioner. In the early years of parliamentary enclosure larger numbers, as many as twenty or more, were appointed, particularly in Lancashire and Gloucestershire – probably to confer greater respectability on the procedure, though only a few practical members might do the actual work. The shortage of reputable surveyors meant that most Commissioners were large owner-occupiers or substantial tenant farmers with a good knowledge of local farming and perhaps some experience of surveying. Clergymen with some knowledge of farming who could oversee the Church's interest in glebe lands and tithes might also be nominated. It was not unusual for the agents of leading proprietors to be involved – Thomas Davis, Lord Bath's agent, served as Clerk to the Commissioners in the Cheddar enclosure of 1795 (incurring personal expenses of nearly £400) – and it was not until 1801 that Parliament adopted a standing order which laid down that no lord of the manor, or steward or bailiff of a proprietor, could act as a Commissioner in any enclosure in which he or his employer was an interested party.[27]

Once Commissioners became known for satisfactory work they were employed time and again within a certain district, and some became virtually professional Commissioners, spending much or all

25. Wilts. RO: Longleat Box 16.
26. David J.V. Jones, *Before Rebecca: Popular Protests in Wales 1793–1835*, 1973, p. 41.
27. Wilts. RO: Longleat Box 23; Hammond and Hammond, *Village Labourer*, p. 39.

of their time on the work. Some began as surveyors for enclosures and graduated to becoming Commissioners, perhaps continuing with some surveying work as opportunity offered. Chapman cites the example of Edward Hare of Castor who served as Commissioner in as many as 133 enclosures, and as surveyor in a further number. Hare's work as a Commissioner involved him in the enclosure of over 273,000 acres, while John Dugmore, employed in 135 enclosures, was responsible for nearly 259,000 acres. The average distance travelled from home by Commissioners was less than 20 miles, a natural result of being chosen for local knowledge; but also, given the often protracted nature of the work, a consequence of the need to keep down time and money spent in travelling, since Commissioners were paid by the day. One result of this was that a relatively small number of persons made a quite profound effect on the appearance of the local landscape as new hedges and fences divided up the former open fields and commons into a pattern of small enclosed fields.[28]

Copies of the Act having been sent to the Commissioners, preferably in time to allow them to make some progress before the onset of winter, they gathered for their first meeting in the parish to be enclosed or very nearby. Usually they met in the village inn, where they could stay overnight and, if necessary, continue their meeting on the following day. Thus we find Thomas Davis, Junior, appointed a Commissioner for the Backwell (Somerset) enclosure, writing to the Clerk on 4 June 1807 to propose a first meeting for the following 3 August:

> I presume it will be adviseable for us to remain at Backwell a Day or two to make a general view of the parish and direct the Survey. We shall leave it to you to order a Dinner on that Day at 4 p.m. I understand there is an inn at Backwell. I hope there are good beds, but at all events you must contrive where we shall sleep.[29]

In the case of the Kingston Deverill enclosure, where Thomas Davis, Senior, was Clerk to the Commissioners, a notice fixed to the door of the parish church on 30 June 1782 announced the Commissioners' first meeting, and it was also advertised in the leading local newspaper, the *Salisbury and Winchester Journal.* At this first meeting, on 17–18 July, the bounds of the parish were perambulated, and a surveyor appointed to map the existing holdings, and subsequently

---

28. John Chapman, 'Enclosure Commissioners as Landscape Planners', *Landscape History*, XV, 1994, pp. 52–3. For details of surveyors, see Peter L, Hull, 'Some Bedfordshire Surveyors of the Eighteenth Century', *Journal of the Society of Archivists*, I, 1955, pp. 31–7.

29. Wilts. RO: Longleat MSS. 845.

to stake out the new allotments and roads at a fee of 18d per acre (9d per acre for the old enclosures of more than four acres), 10s 6d a day for attending on the Commissioners, and expenses when attending on proprietors making exchanges and alterations to their allotments; he was also to receive 'reasonable satisfaction' for making maps. Thomas Davis's bill for obtaining the Act, only £265 13s 4d (no solicitor was employed), was agreed, and the sum of £200 was borrowed by the Commissioners from a certain Simon Jude Cole of Honingsham in order to meet current expenses.

At further meetings on 9–11 September and 26 September the Commissioners valued the lands, and on 28 September and 4 November 'schemed out' the roads. At four meetings between 24 October and 7 November claims to receive allotments were considered, and the survey was read out to the owners and objections to it heard. On 17 and 18 December the new allotments were 'schemed out', and a rate (or owners' contribution) of £1,052 15s was levied to meet expenses to date. The next meetings, between 3 and 5 February 1783, were of particular importance: the Commissioners heard objections to the new allotments; instructions were given for the husbandry of the open fields pending their enclosure, and notice given that rights of common were to cease on 5 April; and Lord Weymouth, a principal proprietor, was permitted to borrow £433 on the security of his allotment. There was then a lengthy delay while allotments were adjusted to the owners' satisfaction, and it was not until 27–29 June 1785 that the draft award, giving final details of new allotments, was read and agreed. On 23 August 1785 the Award was engrossed, that is, written out in legal form.

Up to the point of laying out the new allotments the process had been exceedingly expeditious, taking only five months. But then followed a lengthy hiatus while proprietors made objections to the proposed allotments and bargained between themselves, exchanging and selling parcels of land to achieve holdings more to their liking. And after the Award was finally agreed there was another delay of nearly three years before the Commissioners were able to end their work, on 27 May 1788, by examining the accounts for the roads and other outlays. The public costs proved to be moderate, only £923 18s for the Act and the Commissioners' and surveyor's fees and expenses, and a mere £163 8s 9d for roads, a total of £1,087 6s 9d.[30] (There were of course additional private costs to be met by owners in respect of fencing their new allotments and making

30. Wilts. RO: Longleat Box 16.

compensation for trees and farming outlays left by the former owners
of their new holdings.)

In a perhaps more typical enclosure, that of Hanworth, near
Sunbury in Middlesex, the Commissioners' meetings stretched
from 20 August 1800 to 21 April 1803, when the revised Award
was completed. More than fifty meetings were held in this period,
and subsequent meetings were also necessary in order to hear
complaints, answer letters, inspect and settle accounts, and issue
warrants of distress against those owners who had failed to pay for
the value of the timber and husbandry work done on their new
allotments. These debts were still not settled as late as the summer
of 1806, more than six years from the date of the Commissioners'
first meeting. The numerous meetings held before the Award was
agreed were for the usual purposes, to receive requests regarding
the location of holdings, to hear objections to the lines of new
roads, the giving of instructions to contractors for the building of
roads and a bridge, and for making a decision on which parts of
the waste were to be sold in order to help meet the costs of the
enclosure (sales of 126 acres produced a total of £2,713). Some
considerable delays arose when owners sold and exchanged lands
before the Award could be completed.[31]

Commissioners were frequently blamed for any unusual delays
in completing an enclosure, and certainly some well-known Commissioners were so much in demand that delays were inevitable
while they were conducting several enclosures at once, and even
attending two separate meetings on the same day. Sometimes
pressing harvest work in summer or bad weather in winter were
responsible for the postponement of meetings, and occasionally
Commissioners failed to attend because of sudden illness or other
reasons. One of the Commissioners for the Husborne Crawley
(Beds.) enclosure excused his non-attendance by claiming that
notifications of the meetings had not reached him or that he was
having trouble with his horse.[32] It was widely suspected that since
Commissioners were paid by the day and were usually allowed
expenses they deliberately dragged out the proceedings and felt
no particular urgency to complete the business. But Thomas Davis,
Senior, who had considerable experience of the matter, stoutly
rebutted such criticism:

31. British Library, Egerton MSS. 2355. For a detailed account of an enclosure
concerned with commons and waste, see Geoffrey W. Ridley, 'The Inclosure and
Division of Certain Wastes and Commons in the Manor of Hexham', *Archaelogia
Aeliana*, 5th ser., II, 1974, pp. 213–23.

32. Beds. RO: X 21/136–9.

I answer that Men who are chosen as Commissioners, in consequence of their known integrity, as well as knowledge of the Business of Inclosure, will, *for their own Sakes*, if they expect to be employed again, put the parties to as little Expense as possible – but it is the Disputes of Proprietors in some Instances, and a Delay of consenting to Exchanges in others, which procrastinate the Completion of Inclosures – and not the Delay of Commissioners themselves – except indeed such Commissioners who are resolved to get on right or wrong.[33]

Apart from the problems cited by Davis, Commissioners not infrequently found themselves held up by the thorny difficulty of deciding the validity of claims to common rights. One means of testing this was to ascertain if the claimant had sufficient land of his own to support a cow or other stock over winter, it being argued that, otherwise, there could be no question of his having a right to graze stock on the common in summer. In doubtful cases commissioners applied the test of 'time out of mind', that is, they required evidence that the claimant had kept stock on the common for as long as anyone could remember. To this end they consulted elderly inhabitants on the question. In the course of the Westbury (Wilts.) enclosure, for example, the Commissioners were concerned to ascertain the validity of claims to rights on Westbury common made by people living not in Westbury itself but in the nearby hamlet of Bratton. One of the persons interviewed was a certain William Hearn,

aged 80 and upwards who came to Bratton 74 years ago – worked on Bratton Farm 64 years and has since kept a Turnpike gate. Mr John and Mr Henry Drewett then occupied Bratton Farm – at that time and ever since the Tenants of that farm and all the Commoners in Bratton used to stock their cattle on Westbury – turning them in at Heywood Gate – He never knew any obstruction. . . .[34]

In the Kesteven division of Lincolnshire Dennis Mills found that claims to common rights often occasioned difficulty, and in the instance of Skellingthorpe, where there were also disputes over drainage and disagreements among the Commissioners, there was an exceptional delay, the Award not being finally enrolled until 1830, twenty-four years after the work of enclosing had been commenced.[35]

Among the complexities of the Commissioners' task was the confusion which sometimes arose over tithes and tenure. For example, it might prove to be the case that not all the lands involved paid

33. Wilts. RO: Longleat MSS 845, letter to Nathaniel Barton, 3 Oct. 1800.
34. Wilts. RO: Longleat MSS 845.
35. Dennis R. Mills, 'Enclosure in Kesteven', *Agricultural History Review*, VII, 2, 1959, pp. 86–7.

tithes, and that some proprietors already owned the tithes of their lands. A further complication might be that the great tithes were payable to one party, and the small tithes to another. Some old enclosures had rights of common and were themselves subject to common rights; others neither possessed common rights nor were subject to them. Moreover, the problems of re-allocation were multiplied when some owners held parts of their land under one title, and other parts under a different title, as when some land was freehold and some copyhold, while copyhold land might be held under different copies. This may be one reason why the re-allocation did not always result in owners having completely compact holdings in a single location; though sometimes owners preferred their land to be allocated in two or three separate parcels for convenience of access, proximity to roads or farmsteads, the nature of the soils or other reasons.

Examination of a sample of Cambridgeshire enclosures suggests that one reason for unusual delays was sometimes the complexity of the surveyor's task. At Steeple Morden, for example, where over eight years elapsed between the Commissioners' first meeting and the execution of the Award, an exceptionally large surveyor's Bill was incurred because holdings consisted of single lands or strips of less than one acre, and, moreover, many manors were involved, with a variety of tenures, some copyhold, some freehold, some tithe-free, and some not. In 1820, thirteen years after the Commissioners began work, a suit in Chancery was brought against them and the surveyor complaining of excessive charges and inordinate delay.[36] At neighbouring Guilden Morden also the surveyor ran into difficulties, finding the holdings so intermixed that despite 'the assistance of the most intelligent of the inhabitants' it was impossible to separate them.[37]

A common cause of delay occurring towards the end of an enclosure was the failure of some owners to pay the Commissioners' rates. This could delay the execution of the Award by a period of years, as happened at Waresley (Hunts.) where fourteen years elapsed between the Commissioners' first meeting in September 1808 and the execution of the Award in October 1822. Not infrequently it was the large owners who were most backward in paying. General Needham, the chief proprietor at Waresley, was asking in November 1816 for further time to pay, although the Commissioners told

36. Cambridge Univ. Library: Doc. 654, ff. 166, 176.
37. Cambridge Univ. Library: Add. MSS 6044.

him that it was his tardiness which was the principal cause of the
enclosure being so protracted; over two years later he still owed
£922 out of his total rate charges of £2,352.[38] The same proprietor
was also holding up proceedings at Little Gransden (Cambs.) in
1816 – and indeed the problem of getting in unpaid rates was still
delaying the Award there nine years later. With the post-Napoleonic
Wars depression, 1816 was admittedly a bad year for finding payments out of farm rents, and indeed then, and in the previous
year, one of the other owners at Little Gransden explained her failure to pay on 'the more than ordinary Oppression of the Times'
and her unwillingness to distress her tenants for her rents; 'and as
to turning any Property into money *just now* (whilst the whole
Country is looking to Government for relief) I should conceive
nearly impossible . . . .'.[39]

The enclosure of Ulceby (Lincs.) was so prolonged that on 21
January 1832 a number of the owners signed a petition to have it
brought to completion 'as it is now nearly eight years since the Act
was passed . . . and the Act specifies that the Award is to be depos-
ited in the Parish Church within four years from the passing of the
Act'.[40] As might be expected, it was disputes between owners and
Commissioners over claims, and owners' dissatisfaction with their
allotments, that caused the Commissioners most headaches and
also contributed substantially to delays. At an early stage owners
were asked to indicate their preference in the situation of their
allotments: many, especially the smaller owners, wished their allotments to be sited conveniently near their homes, sometimes asking
for very specific locations; others were concerned with access to
roads or water (particularly in the instance of a professional gar-
dener at Guilden Morden); still others were more interested in
having a good quantity of land rather than its being in a certain
place or of high value; and, quite often, larger owners asked for
divided allotments in two, three or more separate pieces, perhaps
to take advantage of different kinds of soil, or for other reasons. At
Ulceby a Richard Maltby complained that his allotment was too
small and placed too far from his home: 'Gentlemen I think myself
very much wrong'd by the inclosure. Therefore I beg you take my
case into consideration, and make me some restitution which would
be thankfully received.' The vicar, too, was annoyed that his allotment was not equal in extent and quality to what he was promised,

38. Cambridge Univ. Library: Add. MSS 6088.
39. Cambridge Univ. Library: Doc. 636, ff. 56, 63, 71, 200.
40. Lincs. RO: Stubbs MSS 24/11/11.

and was also too far from the church, was intersected by occupation roads, and too much taken up by the fencing, which, he said, was not constructed of good materials.[41] At Weston (Notts.) the Commissioners faced a dispute when the freeholders objected to the vicar receiving in lieu of tithes a farm worth 300 guineas a year laid all together in one piece: in fairness he must, they argued, take his share of the three former open fields and the commons.[42]

John Goodman's objection of February 1796 to his allotment in the Husborne Crawley (Beds.) enclosure was long and circumstantial. The vicar, he complained, had been given the best of the land, while his was 'Poor spewy wet and squeatchy . . . our neighbours all no [*sic*] it bears some straw and Poltry but little Corn and as bad Plowing land as any can be, and no Sward at all.' The land he had given up had

> the most Sward of any farm in the Parish of the Size. I allways could cut Forty tuns of Hay Every Year and the rent of it has been for thirty Years at Eighty Pounds a Year. . . . I hope you Gentlemen do not desire to hurt me. I am well assured the Duke [of Bedford] does not. For to my knowledge I never done any thing to Offend the Duke or You. . . . Please to excuse my scrawle as I am very ill, can neither ride or walk, should have come if I could.[43]

No doubt the complaint that the Commissioners received in 1752 from one of the farmers at Witham on the Hill (Lincs.) was one that recurred many times across the country. The farmer had been promised, he said, that he could have his allotment where he chose, but in fact he was obliged to accept the Commissioners' decision; as a result he felt aggrieved at having to pay his share of the costs for 'someone else's enclosure'.[44] The acceptance or rejection of doubtful claims was also bound to create dissatisfaction among owners in a great many enclosures. The problematical nature of some claims to common rights was well exhibited at the Fulbourn (Cambs.) enclosure. Here the Commissioners were confronted with claims from owners of houses that had formerly been barns. That of a certain James Farrant was allowed, although several owners objected, the Commissioners finding that although once only a barn, the property was described as a house in a conveyance of 'about a Century ago', and the occupier had been accustomed to keeping stock on the common. A similar claim was disallowed,

41. Lincs. RO: Stubbs MSS 24/7/69/71.   42. Notts. RO: Ma B. 275.
43. Beds. RO: X 21/98.   44. Lincs. RO: 3 Anc. 7/1/32.

however, when the claimant admitted that his house had formerly been nothing but a barn. Claims were even made by owners of the *sites* of former houses, but the Commissioners rejected these for lack of proof that the houses, when standing, ever possessed common rights. Other claims were rejected on the ground that the houses in question had no homestalls or old enclosures attached to them, and so the occupiers could not have kept stock over winter. And in a case where a tenement had been divided the Commissioners would allow only one common right and not two.[45]

The division of the commons and waste often gave the Commissioners a great deal of trouble. They might face claims, for example, from a canal company whose canal crossed the land in question, or from the Overseers of the Poor whose workhouse had been in the habit of cutting turf for fuel. Existing encroachments, often made without the permission of anyone in authority, might be very numerous and extensive, stretching from 'a small part of a garden' to 'a neat Cottage with stable, piggery and garden, well fenced in'. Rather than have valuable houses and farm buildings pulled down the Commissioners sought agreement between the parties involved on suitable exchanges or compensation.[46]

It was not only the owners who complained of what they saw as unfair and inadequate allotments. Tenant farmers also were involved, since the Commissioners were responsible for re-siting their farms, making compensation for unexpired leases, and sometimes fixing new rents. At Little Gransden (Cambs.), for example, a tenant was aggrieved that after putting a lot of effort into improving the farm he had given up, he now found himself saddled with another farm that needed a great deal of improvement.[47] The lines of new roads to be built by Commissioners, and the stopping up of old ones, were also very frequent sources of dissension, some complainants taking their objections to the Justices at Quarter Sessions. Sometimes brooks and streams had to be diverted to clear the way for new roads, occasionally the road surveyor or contractor was negligent or incompetent, and not infrequently delays were caused by the poor state of the new roads and the refusal of the Justices to issue a certificate that they were satisfactory.

In January 1796 five of the owners at Husborne Crawley signed an objection to the proposed lines of new roads. One of these, it

---

45. Cambridge Univ. Library: Add. MSS 603, ff. 23, 24.
46. Hants. RO: 50M 63 Box 2; 11M 49/465; 25M 58/244.
47. Cambridge Univ. Library: Doc. 636, f. 219.

was urged, would be expensive to build because it passed through some old enclosures, while 'the old road, having a sound and firm bottom, could (if widened where encroachments have been made upon it) be made at a very moderate expense . . .'.[48] At Bassingbourn (Cambs.) it was objected that the new roads would be little shorter than the old ones, and not as easy to repair, while at Ulceby (Lincs.) villagers petitioned the Commissioners to retain an old footpath which ran across the old enclosures.[49] There was, however, some appreciation of the Commissioners' efforts: at Longstow (Cambs.) there was satisfaction that the roads of the parish used to be 'in so deplorably bad a state as to be a horror to the boldest foxhunter while at present the most delicate lady may travel over them without having her nerves shook'.[50]

From these few examples it may readily be understood how difficult and delicate was the Commissioners' task. To please one proprietor they must annoy another; to meet one grievance make another. The interest of the tithe-owners, or that of the major proprietor, might well prove to be at odds with that of the other owners; and if the tithe-owner or major proprietor were a person of rank and importance one cannot but suppose that his interest was likely to be treated with greater consideration. When individual Commissioners represented different interests, one the chief owner, another the tithe-owner, and the third the remainder, as was often specified in the Act, then the result might depend on the authority and personality of a particular Commissioner. Two of the Commissioners, each representing a major interest, might continually outvote the third, who represented the lesser owners. The fear of this happening when three major owners were involved was sometimes an obstacle in agreeing to an enclosure in the first place.

There were also wider interests which might well receive less consideration or be totally disregarded – the interests of those who owned no land but possessed merely a common right, the well-being of the tenant farmers, of the cottagers and the poor, and the village community as a whole. The Commissioners, it has to be remembered, represented property owners in dealing with landed property: their remit was normally no wider than that, and they could not legally go beyond the authority of the Act which empowered them. So limited were their powers that on occasion a second Act had to be obtained for the same parish where it was found that the first

48. Beds. RO: X 21/259.
49. Cambridge Univ. Library: Doc. 623, f. 107; Lincs. RO: Stubbs MSS 24/8.
50. Cambridge Univ. Library: Doc. 645, f. 122.

was inadequate or unsuitable. Thus a second Act had to be obtained, for example, to allow the Commissioners to use ditches as divisions rather than fences (for example, where the fences were being destroyed by rioters), or to avoid having to sell part of the waste in order to defray the costs where the owners found it preferable to retain all the waste.

It is not to be expected that the Commissioners could always achieve a fully satisfactory result, or that in many instances some owners, and notably the owners of common rights, might not think themselves cheated out of property that perhaps had been in their family for generations. Often the justice of the Commissioners must have been rough justice indeed. But, in general, they seem to have been honest and upright, and as fair as circumstances allowed. Certainly their fairness seems to have been widely accepted, and the impartial nature of their role was set out in the following letter, one written in 1812 by a friend to an owner who was unwilling to accept his allotment:

> I hope you will not be afraid of talking to Jackson one of the Commissioners, he is bound to do you Justice and not to listen to one Proprietor more than another. I look upon him to be a Servant to the Proprietors for whom he is acting and ought to listen with the greatest attention and care to every one of the Proprietors who may think themselves aggrieved, and remove the Causes of Complaint as soon as possible.[51]

Of course, the Commissioners did not escape criticism. In 1770 Arthur Young included an extended attack on the enclosure process in his *Northern Tour*.[52] He criticised, in particular, the 'despotic power' of the Commissioners, their 'carelessness and partiality' in making allotments, the lack of adequate public scrutiny of their accounts, and the difficulty of securing redress, except through the costly and time-consuming means of filing a Bill in Chancery, a remedy perhaps 'as bad as the disease'. Young was writing as the first great upsurge of parliamentary enclosure, that of the fifteen years after 1765, was gathering pace, and before the work of executing enclosures had become as regulated and open to public scrutiny as it was soon to become, and before numbers of Commissioners had attained high reputations for probity and skill in carrying it out. Nevertheless, there were valid criticisms to be made. The

51. Cambs. RO: P 139/28/12.
52. Arthur Young, *A Six Months' Tour through the North of England*, 1770, I, pp. 252–64.

Commissioners did indeed have great powers of disposing of private property; they may not always have acted in an unbiased manner; they did ignore the needs of the rural poor, except in the limited instances where they were specifically instructed in the Act to provide cow pastures for their cattle or allotments vested in trustees to provide fuel; the costs incurred were sometimes higher than was strictly necessary; and there was no effective means of challenging their decisions except by resort to law (later Acts allowed appeal to Quarter Sessions), when it was often too late in any case.

To modern historians the greatest weakness was the infrequent (and often inadequate) provision for the village poor. This is a subject to which we must return in Chapter 7, but here it should be pointed out once again that Commissioners could only execute what was in the Act, and the Act was a creation of local landowners almost always concerned solely with a reorganisation of private property and not with the good of the village community at large. Further, rural poverty was a matter for the Justices and parish authorities operating under national poor laws, and in the majority of villages did not become an urgent issue until the era of high food prices that set in with the French Wars after 1793. The Commissioners' work was no doubt imperfect: they might not have been as impartial as their task required, and they might sometimes be laggardly and inefficient, occasionally even corrupt. But, taken as a whole, the evidence suggests that they discharged a complex and difficult duty with a large degree of competence and such fairness as their remit allowed.

CHAPTER FIVE

The Gains of Parliamentary Enclosure

Farming gains

From the landlords' point of view the principal gain to be obtained from enclosure was the increased value of the property, which made it possible for them to charge a higher rent for it. Often, at the same time as the land was enclosed, the new situations of the farms necessitated the provision of new farmhouses and farm buildings, such as barns, stables, cowsheds, pigsties and yards. These required further investment on the landlords' part, but also enhanced the value and rent of the property. Even where it was still possible to make use of existing farmhouses and buildings, the opportunity might be taken of making improvements or even completely re-building where they were in a 'most ruinous and dilapidated state', replacing them in a 'substantial and handsome manner'.[1] Further money might also be spent on additional improvements, such as drainage of wet soils, the building of embankments against flooding by river or sea, and the provision of farm access roads.

From the tenant's point of view, the major improvement, in addition to new buildings or drainage, was that he now had a much more compact farm, subdivided into fields convenient for adopting more complex rotations of crops, or for more efficient breeding and fattening of stock, and for dairying. In the large number of enclosures which resulted in the provision of new parish roads, the fetching of seed, manure and soil dressings, and carrying crops and driving stock to market, were all made easier. Further, reorganisation of the old enclosures helped enhance their usefulness, while commutation of the tithes was a major advance which increased the value of the farms both for landlords and for tenants.

1. Report on enclosure of Coldeaton, Derbyshire.

We should remember, however, that not all enclosures resulted in better parish roads, modernisation of the old enclosures or commutation of the tithes. It was not always the case, either, that after enclosure the farms were entirely compact or always conveniently located. Landowners quite often requested the Commissioners to allocate their land in two or more separate pieces, and where this was not requested by the owners the Commissioners may have been obliged in some instances to sacrifice compactness to their legal responsibility of sharing out the good and poor soils. It appears that the small owners, who usually requested their allotments to be located near their existing houses (which were often in the village centre), received priority, and it was the larger owners who had to accept allotments further from the centre and perhaps on the periphery of the parish, and split between two or more separate pieces of land. It was this kind of re-allocation which often obliged owners to provide new farmhouses and farm buildings.

The reasons why the larger owners sometimes requested divided holdings were various. One was to have soils possessing different characteristics, since soils often varied considerably in type and quality even within the limits of a single parish. Another might be to take advantage of existing farm buildings or fences and avoid the expense of providing new ones; or perhaps to retain land that had long been in the hands of the family. Dr Chapman has suggested that where an individual owner had claims to shares of both the field land and the common, Commissioners might have been anxious to avoid controversy and complaint of partiality by making separate allocations, one from the former fields and the other from the former common. Similar situations occurred where more than one parish was involved, and owners had rights in more than one common before enclosure. In such cases Commissioners might have been doubtful whether they had the power to allot the land in single blocks.[2] However, perhaps allotment of more than one block in former field land is most likely to have been the effect of ensuring a fair division of the good and poor soils, and of meeting the wishes of proprietors, as explained above.

Where former waste lands were enclosed – and many of the later enclosures, especially in the north of England and in Wales, were concerned largely or entirely with waste – the value of the enclosures for farming was often difficult to assess. Waste land had

2. J. Chapman, 'The Parliamentary Enclosures of West Sussex', *Southern History*, 2, 1980, pp. 80–1.

previously remained uncultivated either because it lay on steep hillsides or was difficult of access, or because the soil was too poor to be worth cultivating when better land was available. The rise in agricultural prices in the later eighteenth century, and especially during the French Wars of 1793–1815, made the enclosure and cultivation of some of this poor land at least an economic possibility. It is not surprising, therefore, that many of the enclosures of waste occurred in this period, while after 1815, when the level of prices fell back to figures not much higher than before the Wars, the poorest of these recently enclosed lands were no longer profitable and were allowed to revert to waste. In the North York Moors the value of the waste was so doubtful that the enclosure Acts did not oblige the owners to fence or wall them in, and in many cases, indeed, such expenditure would not have been justified.[3]

Landowners seeking to attract tenants for farms newly created from the waste were often obliged to involve themselves in large additional outlays, notably for new farmhouses and buildings and access roads. In addition, the problems of reclaiming waste land varied greatly with its situation and the nature of the soils, and might involve very considerable outlays in fencing, hedging or dry-stone walling, as well as drainage, as in the Somerset Levels.[4] Landowners had to offer tenants long leases in order to assure them that their expenditure in breaking down formerly uncultivated soil, removal of brushwood, weeds and stones, and application of plentiful quantities of manures and soil dressings, would be recouped in years to come. Not infrequently a lease for twenty-one years would be broken into three phases: the first during which only a very low rent, or even no rent at all, was required; then a phase of a moderate rent; and lastly one at a full rent for the remainder of the lease when it could be assumed that the land was fully productive. Apart from outlays on improvements, tenants also faced problems with labour. The preliminary task of clearing the land for cultivation was highly labour-intensive, as were the early crops put in to clean the soil, such as potatoes. In the northern and eastern moorlands, heaths and wolds, where waste was often extensive,

---

3. J. Chapman, 'Parliamentary Enclosure in the Uplands: the Case of the North York Moors', *Agricultural History Review*, XXIV, 1976, pp. 1–17.

4. Michael Williams, 'The Enclosure and Reclamation of the Mendip Hills 1770–1870', *Agricultural History Review*, XIX, 1, 1971, pp. 69–70. For the varied problems of waste land reclamation, see also Michael Williams, 'The Enclosure of Waste Land in Somerset 1700–1900', *Transactions of the Institute of British Geographers*, 57, 1972, pp. 105–8, and in the same journal, 'The Draining and Reclamation of the Somerset Levels 1770–1833', 33, 1963, pp. 165–77.

villages were small and scattered, and labour might have to be hired from a distance. It was these conditions which helped give rise to the notorious gang system of the eastern counties, when women and children were employed by gang-masters for such laborious work as weeding and gathering stones. The poorest waste lands, however, were not worth cultivating at all, and so in Wales and parts of northern and eastern England they became fenced-off sheepwalks or merely unfenced 'rough grazings'.

Arthur Young noted an instance of waste cultivation in the Norfolk parish of Cawston, near Norwich. There Colonel Buller, the chief proprietor, owned 1,300 acres of commons and warren. The land brought into cultivation was improved by ploughing and leaving for a year, followed by the sowing of coleseed, fed to sheep: the manure and the treading of the sheep further improved the land. As many as twenty-five loads of marl per acre were laid on in the first year, and in subsequent ones a further ten loads were applied, mixed with clay. Rents of the newly cultivated land, let on twenty-one-year leases, were fixed at between 7s and 8s per acre for ten years, the tenants undertaking all the improvement except for the buildings; after ten years the rents were to rise to between 8s and 10s. The Colonel kept some 70–80 acres in his own hands to be let to small occupiers for their cows; and he planted trees on 321 acres on that part of the former common that had been most eroded by many years' paring of the turf for fuel.[5]

The royal forests of England, such as the Forest of Dean, Exmoor, Sherwood, Rockingham, Salcey and Whittlewood, had been diminished over many years by grants to neighbouring landowners, and by illegal encroachments, both large and small. Many of the trees had been cut down for private use or for sale, and intakes of forest land had been appropriated for small-scale farming by local cottagers, craftsmen and squatters. The royal forest of Delamere in Cheshire is an interesting example of the changes of use made possible by enclosure. By the eighteenth century Delamere was more of a 'vast heathland' than a forest. The nearby townships had long used forest land for common grazing, and in the second half of the eighteenth century Acts were obtained for enclosing the grazings and bringing them into cultivation. Subsequently, in 1812, near the close of the Napoleonic Wars, official concern regarding the supply of oak for maintaining the fleet led to plans for the reclamation of the royal forests as nurseries for timber. Enclosure Acts and

5. Arthur Young, *General View of Norfolk*, 1804, pp. 93–4.

deforestation Acts gave the Crown the sole right of growing timber there. In the instance of Delamere, the enclosure of 1812 resulted by 1823 in the planting of some 3,600 acres, a tenth of the total acreage enclosed in Britain for this purpose.[6] Thus, over a few decades after 1767 the old common grazing of the forest had been replaced by cultivation, and much of the remainder was planted as a national forest reserve for naval use.

There were obvious economic gains where waste land could be transformed by enclosure and subsequent improvement. The resulting increase in rents was sometimes spectacular. Young reported an account of Welby, near Sleaford in Lincolnshire, where former heath land, previously let at a mere 10d per acre, had risen to as much as 10s or 12s after enclosure.[7] Increases on this scale were, of course, exceptional, and generally much more modest figures ruled. It has to be remembered, again, that much waste land was barely worth the cost of enclosing, and, indeed, as was noted above, some enclosed former waste was abandoned in the post-war price fall, while large areas of very poor waste were of such slight value as never to have been the subject of an enclosure.

Enclosure of field lands and their commons was more certainly profitable, although here again the benefit varied greatly from one situation to another. Much depended on how extensive the fields and commons were before enclosure, and to what degree they had been eaten away by earlier piecemeal enclosure. A tiny rump of open field and a small remnant of remaining common would not make very much difference to the way the bulk of the land in the parish was farmed. In general, access to markets, to major towns and to industrial areas with large and growing populations was clearly an inducement to enclose, both to expand the food supply and to obtain land for works, warehouses and housing. Proximity to major roads, navigable rivers and canals, inland ports and coastal harbours might also be influential.

But, for farming, the key factor, as a rule, was the soil. Opinion held that a rich easily worked loam, suitable for growing a wide variety of crops as well as for market gardening, and readily capable of being laid down to grass in leys or temporary pastures, was the most profitable kind of soil to enclose. Near rapidly expanding industrial towns and villages, as in the south Yorkshire district or the Black Country, a soil adaptable to corn, market gardening,

6. E.S. Simpson, *The Reclamation of the Royal Forest of Delamere*, 1970, pp. 272, 274–80.

7. Arthur Young, *Annals of Agriculture*, XVI, 1791, p. 605.

dairying, early vegetables, poultry and fruit was bound to be in demand. In the best situations the value of the former field lands might double or mount even higher, while that of former commons, if on good soils, might multiply three-, four- or five-fold.

At the other extreme there remained in some districts badly drained, waterlogged clays which were difficult and expensive to cultivate, and limited in the uses to which they could be put. It is often supposed that enclosure invariably led to more advanced and more efficient forms of farming, but on some heavy, wet clays this was by no means the case. Enclosure alone could not change the nature of the soil; its great advantage to the farmer was that it gave him greater control over his land and, particularly, over the use to which it was put. He could, if the circumstances were right, drain a heavy soil, expand his arable and produce more of a wider range of crops; or he could convert worn-out arable to grass and concentrate on breeding, fattening and dairying; with the right soils and access to markets he could go in for market gardening, hops or fruit; and generally he could cater more closely for expanding and profitable markets.

However, a heavy clay that had not been drained greatly limited these options, and, moreover, failed to attract the kind of enterprising, moneyed farmers who were prepared to experiment with different modes of farming. On the poorer clay soils, consequently, it was not unusual to find newly enclosed land still being farmed by the former occupiers in much the same way as when it was in open fields and commons. The same traditional rotations of two or three white crops and a summer fallow were still employed, partly because the farmers were unfamiliar with other rotations but more because of the limitations of their soil, while the fallows remained an essential feature for obtaining a periodical clearance of weeds and the restoration of fertility for the following crops.

The county *Reports* to the Board of Agriculture, written at the end of the eighteenth century and beginning of the nineteenth, at the high point of the parliamentary enclosure movement, drew attention to this situation. Bare fallows were continuing in many places after enclosure, and indeed the great agricultural authority, William Marshall, held that summer-fallowing was essential for heavy soils. Sometimes, furthermore, enclosure was followed not merely by unchanging styles of farming but by deterioration, where farmers had taken advantage of their greater freedom of land use but had failed to adjust their system accordingly. In Wiltshire, for example, Thomas Davis noted that farmers had expanded their arable acreage but without taking steps to maintain the fertility of the soil, and had even allowed their flocks to decline.[8]

It is interesting that even where the farmers left their methods unchanged, they were prepared to pay much higher rents than previously for the land. Presumably this was because of the advantage of having land that was no longer subject to common rights (and perhaps also free of tithes), and was completely under their own control so far as its use for farming went. Of course, it may be that one reason for the farmers continuing with their old methods was sheer conservatism, especially perhaps among the older men; and to this unwillingness to take risks might be added a lack of funds with which to meet the cost of converting to grass, buying more livestock, or of employing more teams and wagons where the arable was expanded. The larger farmers might also have had their freedom of cropping restricted by the terms of their leases, although it seems that most leases were more concerned with safeguarding the value of the land and buildings than with a close regulation of the crops that could be grown.

In time, standards of farming did improve, even on the clays. The balance of arable and pasture might change, shifting more towards the latter, making it possible to keep more cattle and sheep, thus achieving a more flexible pattern of output as well as a better manured and more productive arable element. Transport improvements gave better access to town markets and also encouraged farmers to use their returning wagons for bringing back loads of fertiliser, the waste products of breweries and slaughterhouses, for instance, or the 'town muck' or 'night soil' provided by town stables, cowsheds, and house privies and cesspools. But generally the evil reputation of the undrained clays for backwardness and high costs of cultivation (arising from the large teams required and the greater importance of catching the right weather for cultivation) discouraged enterprising farmers from taking on farms in clayland districts, while in periods of low prices these were the areas most likely to be seriously depressed. In some districts the drainage of the clays, indeed, remained a problem until the coming of cheap pipe and tile subsoil drainage from the 1840s onwards; and this, of course, was often half a century or more after they had been enclosed.

8. See William Marshall, *Review of Reports to the Board of Agriculture*, York, 1808–18, esp. III, pp. 49–53, 618; IV, pp. 610–18; V, pp. 381–2; Arthur Young, *Tours in England and Wales*, 1932, p. 204; Arthur Young *Eastern Tour*, I, 1771, p. 24; Thomas Stone, *General View of Bedfordshire*, 1794, p. 26.

Where the soils were more amenable to improvement, the gains in output, and hence in farmers' profits and landlords' rents, could be very substantial. Young noted ten examples in the area around Hunstanton in north-west Norfolk where, he reported, the produce had at least doubled, and the rents, when the farms came to be let for the second time after enclosure, had risen considerably. Prior to enclosure the distance the farmers had to travel to the fields from their village farmhouses was so great as to discourage enterprise. Now that the farmhouses were situated convenient to the farms they had become much more interested in making improvements.[9]

Young made enquiries regarding a number of other Norfolk enclosures and discovered that the changes which had occurred in the farming varied greatly from one place to another. For example, at Carleton, near Norwich, the 1,200 acres enclosed, mainly from the former common, consisted of a sandy loam and had all been converted to corn, increasing the corn acreage in the parish by 50 per cent. The numbers of sheep had been greatly reduced, however, but had improved in quality. On the other hand, at Felthorpe, north-west of Norwich, the soil was discouraging – 'a grey sand on red and white sand' – and proved difficult to improve. There had been only a very little, if any, increase in corn, and little change had occurred also in the numbers of sheep and cows. By contrast, Heacham, on the coast near Hunstanton, boasted a fine loamy sand, and the enclosure of 1780 had resulted in the adoption of a regular five-shift Norfolk management. Corn, cows, sheep and wool had all increased, and the rents more than doubled. And at Fincham, to the south of King's Lynn, the enclosure of nearly 3,000 acres in 1772 had introduced a Norfolk four-course rotation with turnips and clover, while the former fallows had been abolished. The old common was now highly productive under corn, though there many fewer dairies and not so many sheep were kept as formerly. The soil there was described as 'strong good land; some wet and tenacious'.[10]

While the sandy soils of Norfolk, and other light soils like the chalkland areas of Wiltshire, Hampshire and Dorset, encouraged a post-enclosure expansion of corn and fodder crops at the expense of pasture, and a consequent decline in dairying and sheep, in other districts the reverse tendency was evident. In the west and central Midlands, in Leicestershire, Warwickshire, Worcestershire, Northamptonshire, Huntingdonshire and Buckinghamshire, enclosure often led to an expansion of the area under grass. What had long been a major regional specialisation in fattening and

9. Young, *Norfolk*, p. 184.   10. Ibid., pp. 90–1, 103, 105–6, 124.

dairying, in meat production and cheese, was further developed. Just as the extension of corn was encouraged in light-soil areas by the nature of the soils – but also by the long-term rise in corn prices after about 1750, and particularly in the Napoleonic Wars period – so the opposite move to pasture in the Midlands was based on heavier soils and influenced also by the slower rise but greater stability of the prices of livestock products. Sometimes parishes might see combinations of arable and pasture continued, leaning more towards grass perhaps, but now on different land than formerly. For instance, after enclosure in the Vale of Belvoir in Leicestershire, the former field land in the valley bottom was put down to pasture, while commons were ploughed up and cultivation extended up the poorer land and sheepwalks of the hillsides.[11]

Whatever the direction, progress was not always smooth, of course. Where there was mismanagement by landlord or by tenant, enclosure could have unfortunate effects. The landlord, knowing little of agriculture but told that grass was more valuable than arable, tied his tenants down to having all their land in grass; the tenants, being unused to making pastures and lacking money, did it in the cheapest way, using some rye-grass, clover, and the sweepings of the hay-loft. The result was a miserable apology for a pasture which the tenant was prohibited by his lease from ploughing up. Some landlords again, raising their rents very sharply immediately upon an enclosure, forced the farmers into pursuing a series of exhausting crops, ruinous to long-term fertility, in order to meet the increased demands of the proprietors. Some tenants, on the other hand, intending to give up farming or move away from the parish as soon as the enclosure was completed, deliberately made as much out of their farms as they could in the meanwhile, leaving the unfortunate occupiers who followed them to cope with neglected buildings and exhausted land. And enclosure, of course, did nothing for the farmers' often limited knowledge of their business. Sometimes the farming had to remain unimproved and the rents little altered because the occupiers knew nothing of clovers, rye-grass or turnips.[12]

11. W.G. Hoskins, 'The Leicestershire Crop Returns of 1801', in Hoskins, ed., *Studies in Leicestershire Agrarian History*, Transactions of the Leicestershire Archaeology Society, XXIV, 1948, pp. 131–2.

12. Arthur Young, *Annals of Agriculture*, VI, 1786, p. 460; Thomas Batchelor, *General View of Bedfordshire*, 1808, pp. 243, 246; Arthur Young, *Northern Tour*, I, 1770, p. 261. Further examples of the varying effects of enclosure on farming may be found in Arthur Young, *General View of Hertfordshire*, 1804, pp. 44–9, and Arthur Young, *Annals of Agriculture*, XLII, 1804, pp. 22–57 (Bedfordshire), 318–26, 471–502 (Cambridgeshire), XLIV, 1806, pp. 39–61, 174–201, 288–307, 426–31 (Huntingdonshire).

Nevertheless, contemporary observers like Young noted that valuable changes did occur. In particular, the quality of the live-stock often improved after enclosure. The old open-field sheep, kept mainly for folding on the fields, were replaced by better breeds producing heavier fleeces and more valuable carcasses. The intro-duction of rotations including clover and turnips resulted in finer crops of wheat and barley.[13] In Bedfordshire, however, it was found that the old open-field rotations persisted on the claylands, and at Bolnhurst, a few miles to the north of Bedford, there was an interesting example of some speculators coming to grief after buy-ing up and enclosing a parish with, reputedly, 'the worst soil on this side of the county'. This soil was described as a 'white hard clay, the substratum often blue gault', and the general wetness of the area often made the roads impassable. The new owners had the land turned down to a very poor pasture, and, finding their venture unprofitable, sought to get rid of their unwise investment, keeping the tenants on one-year agreements in order to facilitate a sale.[14]

Post-enclosure changes, whether resulting in an increase in arable or of pasture, or amalgamation of marshland with upland farms, as in Lincolnshire, or in the introduction of convertible husbandry, where the fields of the farm were systematically laid down in turn to grass, then after a period cropped, and then laid down again – all had effects on the farming community. Among the farmers it was those who had the enterprise and capital to make changes who benefited; the conservative, and those lacking resources, failed to prosper and ultimately, perhaps, went to the wall. During the era of very high prices in the Napoleonic Wars, all farmers, probably, whether progressive and efficient or not, could do well, even if some did much better than others. It was at the end of that period, in the post-war depression, that the weaker and less efficient were weeded out. The war period, indeed, may have bene-fited the larger farmers most, for with their bigger output they were able to gain most from the profitable prices; but it does not follow that it was the small farmers who fared worse when prices fell. The larger men had frequently borrowed heavily during the Wars in order to take on more acreage and expand production, and they were caught by the collapse of banks and general restriction of credit that accompanied the fall in prices. Small men with few

13. Young, *Northern Tour*, IV, 1770, p. 339; Batchelor, *Bedfordshire*, pp. 226, 227, 232.
14. Batchelor, *Bedfordshire*, pp. 223, 232.

liabilities and lower outgoings might more easily survive where the big capitalist farmers found they had over-reached themselves.

In large numbers of parishes, however, enclosure had left the farmers with smaller (if tithe-free) acreages than formerly, and it was the men with very small acreages, made even smaller by parting with land to compensate the tithe-owner, who often found post-enclosure survival difficult, regardless of the movements of prices. They might do reasonably well where they could concentrate on dairying or market-gardening, on fruit, eggs and the other small man's specialities, but conditions for these were not always suitable. For corn-and-sheep husbandry, the staple farming of small men over large parts of the country, they might find their reduced acreage of arable inadequate after enclosure, now that it was no longer supported by meadow land and commons for grazing. In Wiltshire Davis noted that small farmers on the downlands tended to lose by enclosure, having now insufficient pasture for keeping the sheep necessary to manure their crop land – a disadvantage which he thought might be overcome by small farmers combining their sheep into one large flock.

Many small farmers, of course, worked the land part-time, as they had always done, supplementing their income by working for the larger farmers or combining their farming with some village craft or trade, such as a local hand craft in the textile, clothing or metal-working industries, or by keeping an inn or running a carrier's business. The effects of enclosure on the availability of local employment varied greatly, depending partly on how much former common and waste land was taken into cultivation, and whether there was an increase in corn growing or an extension of permanent pasture – arable was held to provide twice the employment of the same acreage of pasture. The building of new parish roads and access ways, new farm buildings, and the making and upkeep of hedges and fences all provided additional employment, which helped offset any loss of dairying where the arable was extended, or of field work where pasture expanded. The problem of assessing the overall result is obviously complicated by the endless variety of local conditions, as well as by the general influence of the more rapid growth of the country's population and the considerable migration to towns and expanding industrial areas. At the same time, some rural industries such as iron-making and cloth manufacturing were in decline, while others like clothing, boots and shoes, and metal-working were expanding. We must consider this problem again in Chapter 7, but it is sensible to conclude that enclosure was an influence yielding both benefits and disadvantages for employment; while other factors, both general and purely local, were also having an influence on the supply and demand for labour. Enclosure was indeed an important factor locally – its importance depending on the amount of land enclosed; but it was not necessarily the most significant one, even within the bounds of a single parish.

To sum up, under favourable conditions, enclosure could lead to major advances in farming methods and output: in particular, there were important changes in land use, with the arable area extended in suitable light soil areas, and an increase in pasture at the expense of arable in areas of heavier soils. It has to be borne in mind, however, that conditions for change were not always favourable, and in numbers of places the post-enclosure farming might be little different from that which prevailed previously. There can be no general conclusion that enclosure, by releasing farmers from the limitations of communal farming, inevitably led to major improvements. Of the many factors affecting the outcome, the nature of the soil was probably the most significant. But it would be wrong to argue from this that enclosure in the light soil regions of eastern and southern England was more productive than in the Midlands, where large areas of heavy soils prevailed. Some of the light soils were too thin and too readily drained of nutrients to be very fertile or to be easily improved; some of the Midland clays, on the other hand, could be made to answer for convertible husbandry without the need for improved drainage. Moreover, soils varied widely within regions, even within a single parish. It was not unusual to find a mixture of soils in very close proximity – a fact that may help explain the division and scattering of allotments in an enclosure.

Enclosure might, indeed, result in certain important disadvantages for farming, especially that of the smaller occupiers. Even if the enclosure left the small men with acreages similar to, or, indeed, in excess of, those they held previously, they no longer had the common for grazing a substantial flock, and they also lacked the efficient manuring of the arable by the large-scale communal grazing of the old system. True, it might be open to small men to combine their flocks, as Thomas Davis suggested, but we do not know how often this was done. No doubt, too, small farmers could borrow a neighbour's bull as a substitute for the communal one, and they could still keep a cow or two for milk and butter so long as they could keep part of their land in grass. They might still agree with neighbours to help make up a plough team, and borrow horses, carts and wagons when required. But it is likely that in some instances individual farmers' standards slipped when communal regulation and inspection were removed. Weeds were allowed to flourish, drains left uncleared, and diseased stock permitted to roam. Some farmers undoubtedly took advantage of their new freedom not to improve their farming, but to become idle and slovenly. In general, as mentioned above, small farmers might do best when they could concentrate on dairying or vegetables. But such specialisation demanded a suitable soil and good access to nearby markets, a combination not found very frequently. Perhaps the majority carried on much as before, though now more isolated, more dependent on their own limited resources, than in the old communal system; and consequently they became more liable to failure when disease struck the livestock or pests damaged the crops, or if they themselves became incapacitated by illness or accident.

It is often supposed that enclosure led to important changes not only in farming methods but also in the size of farms. What evidence we have on farm sizes, however, does not support this assumption. It is true that there appears to have been a long-term trend from early in the eighteenth century towards larger farm units with, typically, farms of over 100 acres, and those over 200 acres (the latter considered good middle-sized farms by contemporaries), becoming more common. Small farms of under 100 acres, though remaining numerous, gradually came to occupy a smaller proportion of the total acreage. The change appears to have been independent of parliamentary enclosure since it was happening on some estates well before the period when that type of enclosure was usual, and continued to develop after it. Furthermore, the same trend can be found in parishes that were still open, as well as in those that were old-enclosed (that is, enclosed by agreement before the era of parliamentary enclosure). In fact, it appears to have been a fairly general trend, connected more with estate management than with enclosure of any kind, being associated in particular with the gradual transfer of small farms or parts of farms (that is, closes or individual holdings in the open fields) away from inefficient occupiers who had been managing the land badly and perhaps were falling behind with their rents, into the hands of more efficient ones. In this process old small farm units were broken up and, over a period of time, enlarged ones were established.[15]

15. See G.E. Mingay, 'The Size of Farms in the Eighteenth Century', *Economic History Review*, 2nd ser., XIV, 1962, p. 481; J.R. Wordie, 'Social Change on the Leveson-Gower Estates 1714–1832', *Economic History Review*, 2nd ser., XXVII, 1974, p. 596.

To round off the discussion so far, a major conclusion emerges: we must be careful not to assign to enclosure changes in farming which were certainly occurring, but were occurring not only in parishes where enclosure was taking place but more widely, and over a longer period of time than that taken up by intensive parliamentary enclosure. A major effect of enclosure from a farming point of view was to give farmers greater freedom in their use of the land, and this might well in many instances have led to improved cultivation better suited to the potentialities of the soil, higher standards of livestock, and, in general, greater output. But for a variety of reasons, of which the main one was the nature of the soil, farming methods often changed little, or changed only slowly. Small farmers sometimes found conditions less favourable for them after enclosure, but were helped to survive by the high prices of the later eighteenth century and Napoleonic Wars period. In this respect, enclosure may have encouraged in the long term a growth of larger units, but this was a process that was already occurring, and one that had no necessary connection with enclosure.

Lastly, there is one very important point to be stressed. Despite the presumed, and often real, effects of enclosure on the technical progress of farming, it seems likely that its more important contribution to higher agricultural output came through the bringing into fuller use of former commons and the cultivation of waste lands. According to Chapman's figures, parliamentary enclosure brought into use some five million acres of commons and waste in England and Wales.[16] Admittedly some of this land was of marginal value and was worth cultivating only when prices were at the dizzy heights reached in the war period. Nonetheless, the bulk of it did make a very considerable addition to the country's agricultural resources, meeting the long-held views of contemporary observers who deplored the neglect of potentially valuable stretches of land that were lying idle – until at length they were brought into cultivation by parliamentary enclosure. This new farmland contributed a great part, probably, of the additional food supplies, which helped, along with increased imports, to feed a rapidly expanding population – one which increased spectacularly, by some seven millions, or well over 100 per cent, between 1760 and 1830.

16. J. Chapman, 'The Extent and Nature of Parliamentary Enclosure', *Agricultural History Review*, XXXV, 1987, p. 28.

The measurement of output gains

It is clear from the foregoing that any accurate assessment of the output gains arising from enclosing open fields and commons is very difficult, if not impossible. Much depended on local conditions and particularly on the nature of the soil, as well as the ability and enterprise of the farmers and the willingness of landowners to make further investments in new buildings and drainage after enclosure. There is evidence, derived mainly from the 1801 crop returns, that the yields of grain on enclosed land could be as much as 25 per cent higher than those in open fields, although there is also other evidence that indicates little or no improvement.[17] In considering the 25 per cent improvement in grain yields that could be achieved, it has to be borne in mind that this advance may have been achieved in part merely by the greater flexibility of land use offered by enclosure. Often, old worn-out arable went down to grass, while over-grazed former pastures were ploughed up, producing higher yields than had been achieved on the former arable. In newly enclosed parishes the total area under grass often expanded because farmers had long felt a shortage of pasture under the old system. In consequence, grain production probably became more highly concentrated on the land best suited to it, with favourable results for yields.

There is an obvious difficulty in assessing the improvement in output when arable open-field land and commons were replaced by permanent pasture, and livestock supplanted the former grain crops. The livestock, too, might well be of higher quality, much superior to the nondescript and sometimes poorly fed stock raised on the commons. Under convertible husbandry the effects became more complex because the former open-field output of grain and stock was replaced by a combination of grain and fodder crops, as well as seeing the introduction of improved livestock. Typically, enclosure might lead to an increase in total output for the village as a whole, since the total area under some form of

---

17. M. Turner, 'Sitting on the Fence of Parliamentary Enclosure: a Regressive Social Tax with Problematic Efficiency Gains', paper presented to the Economic History Society, Canterbury, 1983, pp. 39–40. See also M. Turner, 'Benefits but at Cost: the Debates about Parliamentary Enclosure', in George Grantham and Carol S. Leonard, eds, *Agrarian Organisation in the Century of Industrialisation: Europe, Russia and North America*, Greenwich, Conn., 1989, pp. 51–4.

cultivation was expanded by the taking into the farms of the commons and perhaps some pieces of fertile waste. Further, the land formerly set aside in the open fields for access and divisions between holdings was now incorporated into the farms, and may have more than offset the land now taken up by hedges and fences.

Some twenty-five years ago Professor D. McCloskey suggested that the size of the post-enclosure increase in rents would provide a measure of the increase in land productivity arising from enclosure.[18] This was an illuminating suggestion, but unfortunately one difficult to realise. The ascertaining of the size of the post-enclosure rise in rents is by no means a simple task. One difficulty is that the rents paid *before* enclosure were not necessarily an accurate reflection of the productivity of land under the old system. The rents varied, of course, according to whether they were for open-field land or old enclosures, the latter often attracting a rent twice as high as the former. Further, the value of common rights was not assessed separately but was included in the rent paid for the land or house to which these rights were attached. Pre-enclosure rents were also affected considerably by the varying practices of estate management. On some estates valuations were made and rents revised only at very long intervals, which might even be as long as a hundred years; but on other estates new valuations were called for at fairly frequent intervals of every twenty years or so. The rents of some land might therefore be many years out of date when they came to be affected by enclosure. Furthermore, rents of individual farms were frequently adjusted to the circumstances of the tenants, being kept low for infirm or elderly occupiers, and more nearly up to the valuation levels for others.

After an enclosure a prudent landowner might not immediately raise his rents very greatly, allowing his tenants time to settle into their new holdings and absorb the costs of moving, as well as the costs of bringing common or waste land into cultivation. The full post-enclosure rent might not be set until perhaps ten or even twenty years after the enclosure, and again would be affected by the landlord's concern for particular tenants. Moreover, as mentioned above, a rise in rents after enclosure might not reflect any important change in the nature or output of the farming, but merely the tenants' willingness to pay more for the advantage of having

18. D.N. McCloskey, 'The Economics of Enclosure', in E.L. Jones and S.J. Woolf, eds, *Agrarian Change and Economic Development*, 1969, p. 155.

their land in compact blocks, free from communal regulation and common rights, and free also, in many cases, from the obligation to pay tithe. Rents were also affected by any landlord's investment in new buildings and drainage, by transport improvements made after the enclosure, such as the building of a turnpike road, canal or nearby coastal harbour, and by the growth of new market opportunities in developing industrial towns and villages within easy reach. And, of course, rents would also be very greatly affected by price movements. The effects of price movements, and of some other factors, can be allowed for, of course, if sufficient data exist for the purpose, but very often the data are lacking or inadequate. Even the *average* size of the post-enclosure rent increases is not certainly known, although figures exist for individual enclosures. The examples quoted by Arthur Young, with rises of the order of 100, 200 or even 300 per cent or more, can be misleading for the very high figures were no doubt exceptional, and probably referred to successful enclosures of useful waste lands.

McCloskey did make a rough calculation of the increase in national income attributable to enclosure, which was estimated at some £2.1m. a year, or perhaps 1.5 per cent of the national income of England and Wales.[19] There can be but little doubt, however, that the calculation is indeed a very rough one, and rested on assumptions about the average increase in rents, the acreage enclosed and the costs involved which would be open to various objections today. We may never know accurately the dimensions of the economic gains obtained from the modernisation of the farming system over a large area of the country, but there can be no doubt that they were substantial. And, in view of the rapid rise in the country's population which occurred in this period, there can also be no doubt that advantage was reaped not only in economic terms but in social terms also.

We may safely say that for a very large number of enclosures the rise in rents was very considerable, of the order of between 50 and 100 per cent, and much more in some instances of enclosure of waste. After allowing for the costs of enclosure, the net return to the landowner must often have been of the order of 10–20 per cent, which made enclosure one of the best investments of the age – far higher than the return on land purchase (probably only 3–4 per cent net), lending on mortgage (4–6 per cent) or government stock (about 3 per cent), and higher even than in many commercial and

19. Ibid., pp. 158–9.

overseas trading ventures.[20] This makes it difficult to explain the reluctance often shown by landowners to involve themselves in enclosure because of fears of the amount of the costs. Clearly, the costs affected the size of the net return, and the costs in later enclosures (which were often very protracted) could be exceptionally high. Nevertheless, enclosure resulted in a *permanent* increase in the value of the land, and in the long term would normally make the investment very well worth while. Perhaps there were other, more personal reasons for landowners' caution: a shortage of available funds at the time of the enclosure, for example, and possibly a distrust of their fellow proprietors concerned in the project.

It has been argued by Professor Robert C. Allen that before enclosure the open-field rents did not cream off for landowners the whole of the farmers' surpluses; and it is true that except where the soils were of a high quality these rents were often extremely low, usually only a few shillings per acre per annum. Upon enclosure, however, the rents were adjusted to full economic levels, resulting in the redistribution of surpluses away from tenants towards their landlords. The increase in post-enclosure rents, therefore, may be seen as a device for obtaining for landowners a larger share of the total product of the land, and did not necessarily reflect any improvement in efficiency or in output.[21] In this view, rental gains diverted income away from farmers, and may even have reduced their ability to change their farming techniques through shortage of resources; while the increased revenues of landowners went to finance further agricultural investment (possibly in enclosure), or pay for industrial and commercial developments, or merely sustain higher levels of consumption.[22]

Probably, in many instances, the post-enclosure increase in rents represented the effects of a combination of changes. First, no doubt the enclosure was the occasion for a new valuation of the owner's property in the parish and a revision of the rents, in which rents set at low levels many years before were brought up to date. In this respect Allen's point is a valid one. Secondly, the new rents represented a return on the landowner's outlay in bringing about the enclosure, a return which tenants were usually willing to pay since it brought them the advantages of compactness and freedom of

20. M. Turner, 'Productivity Gains and Social Consequences of English Enclosures in the Eighteenth and Nineteenth Centuries', paper presented to the Conference on Agrarian Structures, Montreal, 1984, p. 8.

21. Robert C. Allen, 'The Efficiency and Distributional Consequences of Eighteenth-Century Enclosures', *Economic Journal*, 92, 1982, p. 950.

22. Cf. Turner, 'Productivity Gains', p. 9.

land use, and, often, commutation of tithes. Thirdly, the new rents also reflected any additional landowner's expenditure on new buildings, drainage, embankments and access roads. And lastly, the new rents would reflect, probably after an interval, any advance in productivity – an advance which would be high in the case of waste lands of reasonable quality, but might be quite small or even non-existent where factors such as the nature of the soil limited the possibilities of improved farming.

Of course, whenever rents could be raised to a level that more than covered the cost of the capital investment in the enclosure (reckoned as an appropriate rate of interest on the capital sum involved), landowners gained. But this should not be taken to mean that rents were raised excessively. The level of farm rents depended fundamentally on what farmers were willing and able to pay – not on the landowner's outlays and his desire for higher revenue. Farmers' ability to pay depended in turn on current levels of prices for farm produce, and the actual figure arrived at was the result of bargaining between landowner and tenant, influenced by the nature and location of the farm and the current levels of rents in the neighbourhood. Any landowner who attempted to charge high rents which did not take account of recent price movements, and which were out of line with the level of other farm rents in the district, would soon find himself without tenants.

Insofar as enclosure modernised the structure and modes of farming over a substantial proportion of the country, it made both the owning and the farming of land more efficient and profitable. The level of post-enclosure rents was set ultimately by the demand of farmers for farms, not by landowners' expenditure or desire for revenue. In the process, enclosure may, as has been alleged, have made farming more market-oriented and more capitalistic. But, if so, it merely brought the former open-field and waste-land areas into line with the bulk of the country. And open-field farming itself had always been market-oriented to a degree: farms of 50, 100 or 200 acres were commonplace in most open-field parishes, and farms of this size necessarily produced surpluses which had to be marketed; while there is little evidence that enclosure itself resulted in a marked increase in farm sizes. Of course, this is not to say that enclosure did not have unfortunate effects on many small farmers. In particular, the costs of enclosure, which fell on those farmers who owned land, as well as on large landowners, have long been supposed to have had a fatal effect on many small owners. It is towards these costs, therefore, that we must next direct our attention.

CHAPTER SIX

The Costs of Parliamentary Enclosure

The costs incurred in achieving parliamentary enclosure were not a mere detail of the process. On the contrary: they played a major role in both its progress and its effects. Some owners, large and small, feared the costs would prove so great a burden that they opposed the very idea of bringing a Bill to Parliament. This was especially so where a large acreage was involved, where the proprietors were exceptionally numerous and opposition was expected, and where there were unusual circumstances such as the need for heavy outlays on drainage and roads. For the smallest owners, if they were men of limited means, the fear of burdensome costs might be very great indeed, and might incline them to sell out either before, during or after the enclosure. There is evidence, as we shall see, which suggests that this was a key factor in the large turnover of small owners as a result of enclosure.

However, there is one important point on which we must be clear at the outset: the costs of achieving an enclosure fell *only* on the *owners* of the land and rights concerned, with each owner's share of the costs being proportionate to his share of the total acreage enclosed. It is wrong, therefore, to suppose that the farmers who were not owners paid any part of the costs, although those tenant farmers who as a result of enclosure farmed land in a different location in the parish had to meet their removal and disturbance costs. To repeat, the direct costs of the enclosure fell only on owners, including those farmers who were owners of land; and farmers who were solely tenants were not called upon to pay any share of the costs.

The figures

One element of the costs which owners had to meet was that known as the *public costs*: those incurred in arranging and executing the enclosure, together with any expenditure of the Commissioners on carrying out additional work on behalf of the owners, such as drainage schemes. In addition to the public costs, each proprietor had to meet his own *private costs*, mainly those of ring-fencing or hedging his allotment according to the Commissioners' directions, and of making any necessary internal divisions of his allotment.

The *public costs* included the fees and expenses of the solicitors engaged to draw up the Bill, see it through Parliament and, at the end, draw up the Award. There were also the parliamentary fees; the Commissioners' fees and expenses, including interest payments on sums borrowed to finance the enclosure before the 'rates' or instalments of costs levied on the owners were got in; the surveyor's bill for measuring and staking out the pre-enclosure holdings and the post-enclosure allotments, as well as any work he carried out in connection with new roads, bridges and drainage schemes; the costs of making the new roads, building bridges and undertaking drainage works; and lastly, the outlays on the public fencing, particularly the fencing of the tithe-holder's allotment where the tithes were commuted into land – these fencing costs were borne by the other proprietors.

Figures for the public costs for two counties have been produced by modern research. The figures, which refer to average costs per acre, in shillings, have been brought together for purpose of comparison by Professor Turner, and are shown in Table 1. It is evident

TABLE 1   *Cost of parliamentary enclosure in the eighteenth century in Warwickshire and Buckinghamshire*

	Warwickshire (Average cost/acre in shillings)		Buckinghamshire (Average cost/acre in shillings)	
Pre-1760	11.0	17 Awards	–	
1760–1769	13.7	20 Awards	16.8	10 Awards
1770–1779	19.6	29 Awards	20.6	18 Awards
1780–1789	19.7	6 Awards	24.1	4 Awards
1790–1799	34.08	9 Awards	34.3	5 Awards

Source: M. Turner, 'The Cost of Parliamentary Enclosure in Buckinghamshire', *Agricultural History Review*, XXI, 1973, p. 43.

that while the Buckinghamshire figures are generally higher, the two counties show similar trends. Turner discovered, however, that in a number of instances substantial costs were incurred after the Award was made, so that the figures in Table 1, taken from the Awards, may well under-estimate considerably the true figure for the total public costs. In fact, for four Buckinghamshire enclosures in the 1790s for which post-Award information is available, the average cost was 42.8s, that is, 8.5s or 25 per cent higher than the figures based only on the Awards.[1]

The upward trend of the figures reflects the influence of two main factors. The first of these is the general rise in the price-level in the course of the later eighteenth century, followed of course by a very large price upswing during the French Wars of 1793–1815. The rise in prices (and wages) was bound to have effects on a number of the costs, notably those for fencing, road-making and drainage. Another factor was that as Commissioners, surveyors and solicitors became better known for their success in enclosure matters they began to charge higher fees, ones more commensurate with their knowledge and status.

The second and more important of the upward influences on costs was simply that as time went by more difficult enclosures were tackled, taking more time to complete; moreover, with time, the objectives of enclosure became more ambitious. Opportunity was taken more frequently to commute the tithes, and there was more extensive building of new roads and drainage of waterlogged fens and marshes – and these were expensive undertakings. Such enclosures inevitably took longer to complete, and even where the objectives were less ambitious Commissioners often ran into delays, (in addition to those caused by their own occasional dilatoriness and failure to attend). For example, in the enclosure of Husborne Crawley (Beds.), completed in 1799, four and a half years after the date of the first meeting, the Commissioners themselves caused postponements when meetings had to be adjourned because only one of their number had turned up. But, in addition, there were occasions when the surveyor failed to attend, while the numerous sales of land and exchanges between the proprietors held up the drafting of the Award. Finally, to cap all, the Justices found the Commissioners' new roads unsatisfactory and refused to grant their certificate of acceptance until improvements had been made.[2]

    1. Michael Turner, 'The Cost of Parliamentary Enclosure in Buckinghamshire', *Agricultural History Review*, XXI, 1973, pp. 39–43.
    2. Beds. RO: X21/126: Husborne Crawley Commissioners' Minute Book.

Taking the various elements in the public costs individually, a great deal of contemporary ink was expended over the size of the parliamentary fees which the proponents of an enclosure Bill had to pay. According to evidence given before a Select Committee of the House of Commons, the usual fees for both Houses on enclosure Bills came to between £170 and £200, including clerks' fees and engrossment. The average fees paid for a total of 707 Bills over the fourteen years 1786–99 were estimated at £169 7s.[3] This sum, while not an inconsiderable one by contemporary standards, was not so great as to form an obstacle to an enclosure where a substantial acreage was involved. It was, of course, much more of a consideration where the acreage was small, and numbers of Bills, it has to be remembered, dealt only with small surviving remnants of open fields and limited areas of common. But in the enclosure of the whole of a large parish parliamentary fees were a relatively minor item, especially when compared with the outlays on roads and fencing. It is only fair to note, however, that amounts recorded in Commissioners' accounts indicate that the parliamentary expenses could be very much more than the average figure quoted above: fees well in excess of £200, up to over £500, were not uncommon, although it is not always clear whether the figure includes the costs of obtaining owners' consents and of bringing witnesses to Westminster to testify to the signatures.

Frequently two solicitors were involved in the obtaining of the Act: a country solicitor who dealt with the proprietors and was familiar with the parish concerned; and a London solicitor whose main task was to see the Bill through Parliament. Either solicitor, or both, might draw up the Bill, and the country man often became the Commissioners' clerk when the Bill passed into law. In that capacity he kept their minutes and accounts, and also drew up and engrossed the Award, which was often a very lengthy and expensive document. The country solicitor might also be involved in securing the consents of owners to the Bill, which was sometimes a protracted and troublesome business involving long and expensive journeys. He drew up the Consent document for parliamentary scrutiny, and was responsible for bringing the witnesses to London. The solicitors' fees and expenses could be substantial, depending on the amount of work involved. As an indication, the average cost of soliciting the Acts for five Cambridgeshire enclosures carried out

3. Report from the Select Committee of the House of Commons on Bills of Enclosure, *Annals of Agriculture*, XXXV, 1800, pp. 363, 392–3.

between 1800 and 1820 was £256, while the clerk's fees came to considerably more at £383, making a total of £639, a very large sum for the time.[4] Solicitors who specialised in enclosure business, like Commissioners and surveyors, often did very well out of it.

The Commissioners and surveyors (some Commissioners acted in separate enclosures as surveyors) also did well out of the work, particularly as they were often engaged on several enclosures at one time. The surveyor, however, if not also working as a Commissioner or surveyor elsewhere, was often a local man whose enclosure engagements were limited. In the early nineteenth century, when the fees had risen from eighteenth-century levels, the bill of an individual Commissioner seems to have been about £150–350, depending very much on the length of the proceedings and the number of meetings attended. Surveyors' bills came to even larger sums, from £300 up to over £1,000, though from the total the surveyor had to pay for his assistants and sometimes, in addition, specialist 'quality men' who valued the different kinds of land involved. By the time of the French Wars the surveyor's basic fee for measuring was at the rate of ls 6d or ls 9d per acre; on top of this he charged for his assistants and for staking out the allotments and roads, drawing plans and attending at Commissioners' meetings. Not infrequently the Commissioners queried the size of his bill, and the surveyor might respond by pointing to the smallness of the pre-enclosure holdings (which gave rise to much detailed measurement), and difficulties he had met in ascertaining whether the holdings were freehold or copyhold, tithe-free or not, and the extent of the common rights attached to them. The surveyor for the enclosure of Carlton, Chellington and Steventon (Beds.) wrote in January 1805 a long letter complaining of the Commissioners' reduction of his bill: he pointed out as one reason for its size that the Commissioners had allotted and re-allotted the fields three times before reaching final agreement. Furthermore, he reminded the Commissioners:

> Gentlemen, when you have settled your accounts you have done with the business. That is not the case with me, for so long as I live here I must be troubled with the disagreements and quarrels of the owners etc. of Lands in all these Parishes near me – I have been at home about 3 weeks, and have had People from almost every Parish around me. The last Person was Johnson from Carlton who complains of not having his road widened up to Grimescroft. . . .[5]

4. Cambridge Univ. Library, Add. MSS 6058, 6065, 6070, 6073, 6074.
5. Beds. RO: GA 1136/5.

The cost of laying out and making new roads depended, of course, on how many roads were to be built and their length, together with the number of bridges involved. In early enclosures road-building was exceptional, but later it became a quite common feature, and certainly added to the amenities of the parish. From 1781 Parliament laid down standards for public fencing carried out by the Commissioners, and also the requirements for new roads built by them. The width of the roads was specified, and detailed provisions set out for their repair and maintenance. The cost of making the roads was to fall only on the proprietors receiving allotments at the enclosure, and public responsibility for their maintenance began only when the Justices had given their certificate that the roads were fit for traffic, and the certificate had been presented by the surveyor to Quarter Sessions and confirmed by the Justices there.

When the line of a new road had been agreed by the Commissioners and staked out by the surveyor, the Commissioners arranged with contractors for the work. In the instance of Little Gransden (Cambs.) one of the contractors involved was a certain John Morgan who in June 1817 agreed with the Commissioners for part of the work, namely that of laying thirty-two loads (of 24 bushels each) of sand and stones on each chain (66 feet) of the new road, at the rate of £4 12s 6d a chain. When Morgan (who signed the agreement with his mark) presented his bill, it amounted to £598 18s 9d. The plans issued to contractors specified that the crown of the road was to be 12 feet wide, rising to a height in the centre of 14 inches above ground level; the total width of the road was 40 feet Grass verges on each side of the carriageway allowed for the passage of livestock.[6]

Road-building then, as now, was costly, and could easily account for a fifth or more of the total public costs. The outlays were increased considerably when the contractors failed to satisfy the Justices, requiring further work before a certificate was issued. The lines taken by roads were among the more contentious issues of an enclosure. Some proprietors were aggrieved that the new roads did not give direct access to their allotments, and launched bitter complaints at the Commissioners and surveyor. And roads appear to have been one of the more frequent subjects for complaints taken to Quarter Sessions.

The public fencing carried out by the Commissioners, including the fencing of the roads, major boundaries and the tithe-holder's

6. Cambridge Univ. Library: Doc. 636/84, 97, 241.

allotment, could also be a very expensive matter. Frequently the public fencing was the largest single item in the public costs. Much depended; naturally, on the acreage involved, and the length of the roads (which had to be double-fenced). It has been calculated for the enclosure of the Mendip Hills that the average length to be fenced was as much as 6 miles per 100 acres. The usual method of enclosing was to combine wooden fences with quickset hedges; the quicks, planted at the rate of one every 3 inches, grew rapidly to form a thick and impenetrable hedge. The cost of such a hedge grown on a bank was 11s per 20 feet in 1806, compared with 10s for a substantial dry stone wall 2 feet wide at bottom and 5 feet high.[7] Dry-stone walling was clearly to be preferred for its permanence and low costs of maintenance where suitable stone was plentiful, and in some waste-land areas the stone had to be cleared from the fields in any event before cultivation could begin.

Typical estimates for fencing from about the end of the eighteenth century onwards ran at some £2 per chain of 66 feet. At Bottisham (Cambs.), for instance, which was enclosed between 1801 and 1808, the figure was £2 2s per chain for '3 rails of Quarter Finland Battin, Posts and Poles of Oak, 2 rows of quicksets with ditches 3ft 6in. Wide on each side and 2 feet deep'.[8] For any particular parish the cost depended very much on how far the materials had to be brought. Often it was possible to obtain the oak for the posts within the parish, but other wood for the rails, and the quicks, might have to be brought from a distance. Transport costs might even make it far too expensive to use wood available in the landowner's own woods or park. For example, it was calculated that the cost of sawing rails and transporting them from Thoresby, Earl Manvers' residence in Nottinghamshire, to his estate at Hagworthingham, near Horncastle in Lincolnshire, a distance of about 45 miles in a straight line, was as much as £3 6s 8d per 120 rails, including canal lock fees and turnpike dues.[9] In a rather exceptional instance of a lowland agricultural parish finding fencing a problem, the Act for Houghton Regis, near Dunstable in Bedfordshire, allowed fencing to be optional, there being doubt whether hedges could be raised there 'and the great price of fencing and railing, and scarcity of wood throughout the said parish and vicinity thereof'.[10]

7. Michael Williams, 'The Enclosure and Reclamation of the Mendip Hills 1770–1800', *Agricultural History Review*, XIX, 1971, pp, 72–4.

8. Cambridge Univ. Library: Add. MSS 6024.

9. Nottingham Univ. Archives, Manvers MSS Ma B433.   10. Beds. RO: B112.

The ring-fencing of the tithe-holder's allotment at the expense of the other proprietors, although a standard feature of the Acts, was a source of some bitterness because of the high cost involved. An allotment of 200 acres required about 2 miles of fencing if it were to be completely ring-fenced, at a cost in the early nineteenth century of about £360. Fortunately, there were often existing hedges or fences that could be utilised to reduce the expense. Ring-fencing, free to the tithe-holder, together with the reduction in the size of other owners' allotments to provide his allotment, was among the very generous terms that tithe-holders were able to extract from landowners anxious to be rid of the tithes, and no doubt contributed to the wave of anti-clericalism which spread across the country in the period of parliamentary enclosure.[11]

Lastly, outlays for drainage, most commonly undertaken in enclosures of marshes and fens, were a major expense in those projects. At Wimbleton (Cambs.), for example, in 1792 the Commissioners were involved in building embankments and making drains, and also erecting pumping engines, for an outlay of some £2,000. To meet this they made a charge upon the owners of a 'drainage and banking tax' of 27s per acre for the first two years after the work was completed, and subsequently set a rate of about 3s per acre for maintenance.[12]

Before leaving the subject of the public costs, it is important to mention that the total bill to be shouldered by owners was sometimes substantially reduced, or even completely paid off, by sales of land. In about a quarter of the Acts the Commissioners were authorised to sell parts of the allotments (including former commons and waste) in order to help defray expenses. The practice was particularly marked in areas outside the Midland region. Study of these sales has shown that a considerable proportion of the purchasers of this land, in addition to local landowners and farmers, consisted of tradesmen and craftsmen from both the parish and neighbouring towns and villages.[13] Enclosure gave such 'outsiders' a rare opportunity for adding to existing holdings (many tradesmen and craftsmen held some land, and a number were part-time farmers) or of setting up a son in business as a farmer, or simply making a secure investment of surplus funds. As a result, ownership

11. See Eric J. Evans, 'Some Reasons for the Growth of English Anti-Clericalism c.1750–c.1830', *Past and Present*, 66, 1975, p. 97.

12. Arthur Young, *Annals of Agriculture*, XLII, 1804, pp. 325–6.

13. John Chapman, 'Landownership and Enclosure', paper given at a conference of the Agricultural History Society, Leeds, 1 December 1990.

in the parish became more diverse and, possibly, new forms of enterprise appeared in a traditional farming community.

A disadvantage of land sales was that in consequence the post-enclosure holdings were necessarily smaller. In some cases this resulted in small holdings being reduced to an uneconomic size, which may have encouraged small owners to sell out. On the other hand, the accompanying reduction in the public costs may have enabled some small owners to meet their share of the costs without having to resort to borrowing or to selling part of an already small allotment. Where the sales of land were made from large areas of former common or waste, the post-enclosure holdings of good farm land would often still have come out at a reasonable size. In any event, the amount of land sold by the Commissioners was often quite small. In fact, they found that purchasers were not always easy to find for large blocks of land: much of the demand was for small parcels, and hence it was better to keep the sale allotments small and preferably on sites near the centre of the village in order to attract local buyers like farmers, tradesmen, craftsmen, builders and professional people.

Dr Chapman's research into Commissioners' sales in West Sussex enclosures found that the area of land sold was not usually very large; in fact it represented on average just under 15 per cent of the area enclosed. In three of twenty enclosures in which sales were used as a means of meeting the costs, the amounts were under 10 acres. Most of the purchases were made by local landowners and farmers, while tradesmen and craftsmen were much in evidence for the small parcels, along with professional men, a few builders, and even an occasional labourer.[14]

The *private costs*, falling on individual owners, consisted primarily of the requirement to ring-fence the allotment and subsequently, if desired, to make internal divisions. Again this could be expensive where it was not possible to take advantage of existing fences, hedges or walls. Internal divisions were often a considerable charge as the preferred size of closes was generally small, mostly ranging between 5 and 15 acres. The ring-fencing of an allotment of 30 acres cost about £160 in the early nineteenth century, and two internal divisions to make three 10-acre fields cost a further £40. For a large allotment situated on the outskirts of the parish it might also be necessary to build a new farmhouse with its appendant stables,

14. John Chapman, 'Land Purchasers at Enclosure: Evidence from West Sussex', *Local Historian*, 12, 7, 1977, pp. 337–41.

barns, cowsheds, and so on. Depending on the scale of the buildings, the cost of this ranged between a few hundred and over a thousand pounds, while cottages for the labourers could be erected for some £40–50 each. Sometimes, to save this expense, old farmhouses or barns were converted to labourers' dwellings.

Lastly, where the allotment had to be reclaimed from the waste, the private costs included both farmhouses and substantial expenses for reclamation. Clearing the land of weeds and stones, ploughing to break up the soil and further destroy the weeds, together with dressings of lime, cost from about £5 to as much as £15 per acre. So although newly enclosed waste was low rented in the early years of a first occupation, the tenant might have to meet initial outlays of perhaps £2,500–7,500 to bring an area of 500 acres into cultivation. Subsequent manuring, drainage and purchases of seed had all to be added to the expense. Necessarily the land had to be considered worth the outlay of such expenditure, and of course it was the high prices of the French Wars period which encouraged much of the enclosure and cultivation of marginal land.

However, for the ordinary middle-sized farmer, having an allotment of, say, 200 acres situated sufficiently close to his existing farmhouse, and already cultivated, it was the ring-fencing which was the major item in his private costs. Two hundred acres, allotted all in one piece, would cost some £200 for ring-fencing alone in the early nineteenth century, without benefit of existing fences but taking advantage of sharing boundaries with adjacent owners. In addition there were the disturbance costs and trouble of moving to the new location. Tenant farmers, as already emphasised, paid no share of the public or private costs, which fell entirely on owners. Tenants, however, did have the costs of removal, and suffered cancellation of any existing leases (for which they were entitled to compensation). A new lease would probably have to be agreed at a considerably enhanced rent; but against this, the tenant now had the advantages of a compact holding, the abolition of common rights, freedom of land use, and perhaps the convenience of a new, up-to-date farmhouse and outbuildings, while also enjoying, very often, improved parish roads and commutation of the tithes.

Before leaving the subject of the burden of costs, it should be noted that, in total, the expenditure of securing and executing parliamentary enclosures represented, for the age, a very large investment of capital in the modernisation of farming. In 1971 Dr B.A. Holderness estimated the capital outlay at £10m. for the public costs, and a further £19–25m. in private capital investment following enclosures. Turner's more recent estimates indicate that the total public costs fell between £6.77m. and £14.34m., with as much again for ring-fencing, making a joint total of £13.5–28.7m. Private expenditure on fencing, drainage and buildings might produce a figure of £27–57m., or perhaps some £10 per acre over the whole period.[15] This was an enormous sum by contemporary standards, especially when it is remembered that parliamentary enclosure affected only something over a quarter of the land area of England and Wales, while the total national income for Great Britain has been estimated at £232m. in 1801, with investment in enclosure accounting for up to about 1 per cent of this figure – a not inconsiderable proportion.

Not all of this huge investment bore much fruit in terms of output and efficiency, as we have seen: some of the enclosed wastes were abandoned after the Napoleonic Wars; some of the drainage had to be done over again at a later date; and in the middle and later nineteenth century post-enclosure hedges and fences had to be removed to create larger fields better adapted for the use of machinery. But the basic change from a communal farming system to one established on the occupier's sole use of the land was a permanent one, and helped lay the foundation for the progressive techniques which distinguished much of English farming in the nineteenth century and after.

Meeting the costs

It has been noted above that in about a quarter of parliamentary enclosures some part of the public costs was met by the Commissioners' sales of land. Frequently these sales met only a small part of the costs, but sometimes it was a substantial part, occasionally even the whole of the public costs. But in the majority of enclosures where there were no sales of land, what were the means open to an individual proprietor for meeting his share of the costs?

15. B.A. Holderness, 'Capital Formation in Agriculture, 1750–1850', in J.P.P. Higgins and Sydney Pollard, eds, *Aspects of Capital Investment in Great Britain 1750–1850*, 1971, p. 166; Michael Turner, 'Benefits but at Cost: the Debates about Parliamentary Enclosure', in George Grantham and Carol S. Leonard, eds, *Agrarian Organisation in the Century of Industrialisation: Europe, Russia and North America*, Greenwich, Conn., 1989, pp. 60–1; B.R. Mitchell and Phyllis Deane, *Abstract of British Historical Statistics*, Cambridge, 1962, p. 366.

The size of his share depended on the acreage allotted, and was proportionate to the share that his allotment bore to the total acreage allotted. On average, over the whole period of parliamentary enclosure, the costs per acre (including ring-fencing, which owners were usually compelled to carry out) has been estimated at between £2 10s and £5. The amount was lower early in the period and higher later on, especially during the French Wars, for reasons already noted. Professor Turner has estimated the average for the public costs alone, without ring-fencing, at between £1 4s and £2 10s.[16]

The large proprietor, having to pay for some hundreds of acres, possibly a thousand or more, clearly had a large bill to meet. But normally he also had large resources to draw upon. He might own an estate amounting in total to several thousand acres and could easily meet his enclosure costs of a small part of it from his rents and other estate revenues, though there was a period of difficulty at the end of the Wars when prices and credit collapsed, and farm tenants fell into arrears with their rents. Alternatively, if all his income were already spoken for, he could mortgage land (provided it were not already mortgaged up to the hilt), or he could borrow on his personal credit. Normally there should have been no problem in his finding the money, although it must be said that large proprietors were often among the most backward in paying up and enabling the Commissioners to settle their accounts.

It is when we come to the other end of the landownership scale that the problem may well have been more acute. The small owner of, say, 20 acres, was faced with a bill for public costs of some £24–50 on the basis of the estimates above, and perhaps as much again for his ring-fencing. What did a sum like £50 mean in contemporary terms to a small farmer? In the later eighteenth century he would be accustomed to paying about £9 for a dozen sheep, £25 for five steers and £28 for four cows – nearly double these amounts during the height of the French Wars inflation. In this period, then, he would pay between £20 and £80 for a small herd. For a quarter (8 bushels) of his wheat he would receive in 1770 £1 19s, and in 1800 nearly £5 13s, and for his barley £1 2s and nearly £3 at these dates. For each 32 1b of his wool he would get some 15s in 1770 and £1 14s 6d in 1800.[17] The annual cash income produced by his land and common rights would have been some £45–50 before the Wars,

16. Turner, 'Benefits but at Cost', p. 60.
17. G.E. Mingay, ed., *The Agrarian History of England and Wales, VI: 1750–1850*, pp. 981, 991.

and more than twice that during the years of high prices. Clearly, in terms of the sums he was used to paying and receiving (as well as lending or borrowing), a sum of £50, even one of £100, would not appear impossibly large.

Further, in a protracted enclosure, where the costs tended to be high, the Commissioners did not demand payment in one large sum but rather raised smaller amounts as they went along, levying a succession of 'rates' on the proprietors. A first rate was levied after perhaps the first year of the enclosure to meet the expenses incurred thus far, a further rate after another two or three years, and a final one for the remaining sum at the end. There might also be a post-Award rate levied to meet expenditure not accounted for at the time of the Award. Consequently, the bill for the public costs was often raised in two, three or more instalments spread over three, five or a longer period of years. This, of course, made it much easier for all the proprietors to pay their bills, and no doubt was particularly helpful for the small owner.

If he could not meet his bill out of current income and savings, there were a number of other possibilities. Like the large owner, the small man could mortgage his land, if it was not already mortgaged to its full value. In 1770 20 acres of moderately good open-field land was worth about £200–250, and if about to be enclosed, considerably more. The interest charge on a mortgage of, say, £100 would be about £5 per annum. Banks were commonplace in country towns by the late eighteenth century, and it may have been possible to obtain a bank loan; but we know very little about farmers' borrowings from banks before the Napoleonic Wars, and probably most bankers would have regarded a small farmer, even a farmer-owner, as an unduly high risk. A mortgage secured on the land, rather than on the farmer's business, was no doubt a much more likely way of borrowing, especially as, if necessary, the owner could obtain the Commissioners' approval of the loan. Borrowing on mortgage was extremely common by the later eighteenth century, and was a secure and cheap means of raising money. It could be done through a country solicitor, but very often was arranged with a member of the family or a friend.

Despite the common use of the mortgage, a much more likely way for a small owner to borrow a sum like a hundred pounds was by a personal loan. Farmers were in the position that at certain times of the year, notably in winter and spring, they were likely to be short of cash, while in the autumn they were comfortably in receipt of money received for their grain and stock. The same farmer might need to borrow at one time of the year, yet be in a position to lend at another. Further, there were in the villages and country towns professional men, tradesmen, craftsmen, widows and others who often had spare funds, and with a banking system that was as yet rudimentary and insecure, they might well prefer to lend at interest to local people whom they knew and trusted. This network of local lending and borrowing has been studied by Holderness, who found it to be already well established early in the eighteenth century, and remarkably widespread and greatly used.[18]

The same impression is conveyed by other sources. For example, in the diary of James Warne, a Dorset farmer, we find him writing in 1758 that on 6 March he received the sum of £20 which he had lent previously on a personal bond, and again on 8 November he received £15 and interest, part of a loan of £30 which was outstanding. At other times he himself was borrowing: on 5 September he borrowed £10 from his father, and on 19 October some friends visited him and offered to lend him money – he thought he might have £40 or £50 from them about Christmas-time. On 20 December, however, he made up his mind to borrow £60 from a Mrs Knapton, a lady living at some little distance, 'on my own Note of hand and I am to give her 4 per cent for it'.[19] This was a very moderate rate of interest, and was no doubt a cheaper and more flexible way of borrowing than by mortgaging land.

Taking into consideration this local network of lending and borrowing between relations, neighbours and acquaintances, spreading perhaps over a radius of 10 miles or so round each village and country town, there appears no reason why most small owners, faced with the costs of an enclosure, could not have borrowed cheaply as much as they needed. Even in bad times when crops were poor or prices low, farmers were able to raise loans, though as a letter of 1755 makes clear, they might prefer to fall into arrears of rent with their landlord, so far as he would permit it. John Bourne, agent of the Lincolnshire landowner William Drake, wrote as follows:

> Y^r tenants that depended on making payments from their wool are disappointed as I thought that they would be. They have raised their money from their friends which they could have done earlier as they are people of credit but they rely too much on your goodness.[20]

18. B.A. Holderness, 'Credit in English Rural Society before the Nineteenth Century with Special Reference to the Period 1650–1720', *Agricultural History Review*, XXIV, 1976, pp. 97–109.

19. G.E. Mingay, 'The Diary of James Warne, 1758', *Agricultural History Review*, XXXVIII, 1990, pp. 74–5.

20. Lincolnshire Archives Office: TYR 4/1/31.

The key words in this letter are: 'they are people of credit'. This was the one condition that was necessary. The borrower's credit must be good – he must be a competent farmer, must not have borrowed already as much as he was worth, and must not have acquired a bad reputation for not repaying his debts. Presumably, those small owners who sold out at an enclosure did so for reasons of bad credit; or because they were left with holdings too small to be viable without common grazing; or because they saw the enclosure as an opportunity for selling out to move elsewhere, or to go into some other line of business, or simply to retire.

A small owner might not be enthusiastic about the enclosure, doubting whether he would get much, if anything, out of it (other than a property more valuable than before). Consequently, he was reluctant to saddle himself with a debt for meeting the costs of a project to which he was opposed. But reluctance to pay must not be confused with inability to pay; and with the facilities that we know were available in the countryside for borrowing, it seems unlikely that any small owner of good credit could not have found the means of paying, if he wanted to do so.

A further ground for coming to this conclusion arises from the structure of land occupation. We know from a variety of sources[21] that a small but not unimportant proportion of small owners farmed rented land in addition to the land they owned. Not infrequently they farmed much more land than they owned, renting perhaps from two or three landlords, and occupying land in neighbouring parishes as well as in the parish in which they owned land. Sometimes the small owner rented out the land he owned and farmed other land that he rented. The point here is that it cannot be assumed that because a man was a small owner in a certain parish subject to enclosure, he was necessarily a small-scale farmer. In a number of cases he might be *a small owner* but quite *a large farmer*. He might also, of course, own land in other parishes, making him a larger owner than he appeared to be in the parish where he was allotted land in an enclosure.

For such owners this puts quite a different complexion on the question of having sufficient resources to meet an enclosure bill – which in fact might be done quite easily out of annual farming revenues. Numbers of small owners were in fact absentees, living, and

21. See G.E. Mingay, 'The Land Tax Assessments and the Small Landowner', *Economic History Review*, 2nd ser. XVII, 1964, pp. 381–8; 'The Size of Farms in the Eighteenth Century', *Economic History Review*, 2nd ser., XIV, pp. 469–88.

possibly farming, outside the parish of enclosure. Some absentee owners lived at a considerable distance, and might not be farmers themselves. The land they owned in the parish of enclosure may have been inherited, while the occupation of the owner was in a profession, in trade, a craft or commerce. Or he or she might be a member of the gentry or retired. Not having any close personal stake in the property they might well decide to sell it when the enclosure occurred; and the enclosure itself, causing a major re-shuffle of the property in a parish, gave an excellent opportunity for profitable disposal.

The turnover of small owners

It is evident from the above that the selling of land by small owners at an enclosure is a complex matter. Not all small owners were small farmers; not all small owners were farmers at all; and not all small owners lived in or near the parish. When small owners sold land it was for one or more of three reasons:

1. to take advantage of the active market in land created by the enclosure itself – to realise the investment, perhaps in order to move elsewhere, take up some other line of business, or retire;
2. because the small owner lacked the credit standing to borrow sufficient money to meet his share of the costs and the cost of ring-fencing: if this were the reason, the owner need only sell a part of his allotment, depending on its size, to raise the necessary amount; and
3. because the allotment after enclosure was too small to be viable for the usual forms of farming. (This might result from the reduction in the total acreage available for allotment caused by land transferred to the tithe-holder and sales of land by Commissioners to defray costs, such losses not being fully compensated by additional land taken in from the commons and waste.)

We have looked already at the first two causes, and we need now to consider the question of reduced size of holdings. Here it is important, in the first place, not to exaggerate the loss of land to provide the tithe-holder with his allotment. The tithes were by no means always commuted into land, and even in parishes where they were, the size of the allotment was not always very great. In Buckinghamshire the proportion of open field and common transferred to the tithe-holder was 20 per cent of that enclosed; in Warwickshire it was 17 per cent. The share of the commons and waste going to the lord of the manor was only 7 per cent, or less.[22] The figure for the tithe-holders' allotments, however, takes into account those parishes in which there was no commutation of tithes into land, and, consequently, in parishes where commutation did occur the figure was considerably higher, probably rising to as much as 25 per cent or more.

If a small man's allotment was diminished by as much as a quarter or more, that certainly puts in doubt the advantage of its becoming tithe-free. But to compensate, and perhaps more than compensate, for the loss of land to the tithe-holder, there was the quantity of former commons and waste to be added to the man's share of the open fields (representing the allowance for the loss of communal grazing and other rights). Overall, it appears unlikely that the small man's allotment was very seriously reduced by the transfers of land at enclosure. Where the waste was extensive and worth cultivating he must have tended to gain. Nevertheless, it is true that in the Midland counties the waste was often very limited, so there he may have come out with about the size of his previous holding in the open fields, or perhaps a little less; but now that acreage was no longer supported by access to a common meadow and commons. Elsewhere, however, he would usually have a total allotment considerably larger than his previous open-field holding.

There is one other point to be made: estimates of the proportion of the total acreage held by owner-occupiers of all sizes run between only 10 and 20 per cent for the end of the eighteenth century; possibly 11–14 per cent might be nearer the fact – we cannot be sure.[23] Whatever the real figure, it was certainly not very great, and furthermore refers to owner-occupiers in general: that for *small* owner-occupiers of, say, less than 50 acres would be lower still. In some parishes, it is true, small owners were certainly numerous and in possession of a substantial proportion of the land, perhaps as much as a third or more;[24] in others they were very thin on the ground; and in some non-existent.

What was generally more important to a small owner than any reduction in the size of the holding was the disappearance of the

22. Michael Turner, 'Sitting on the Fence of Parliamentary Enclosure: a Regressive Social Tax with Problematic Efficiency Gains', paper presented to the Economic History Society, Canterbury, 1983, p. 49.

23. G.E. Mingay, *Enclosure and the Small Farmer in the Age of the Industrial Revolution*, 1968, p. 15.

24. See J.M. Martin, 'The Parliamentary Enclosure Movement and Rural Society in Warwickshire', *Agricultural History Review*, XV, 1967, pp. 27–8.

common. Here, formerly, he could graze his stock when the fields were shut up for the growing crops; moreover, he could look to the village flock to give his crop land a thorough dunging every autumn, in turn with the other farmers. This was the real problem that enclosure caused the small farmer, whether owner or tenant; and the smaller the holding the more he would feel the loss of the common, However, there are a number of considerations to bear in mind. Firstly, it should be remembered that the common did not invariably disappear at enclosure, even if this was the usual outcome.[25] Secondly, a small farmer could often make up the loss of the common by renting additional pasture – and even before enclosure, as we have seen, small owners often rented additional land. Thirdly, it might be open to small farmers to pool their flocks in order to achieve more thorough manuring, but this would not overcome the basic problem unless there was still much pasture left unenclosed or available to rent.

The difficulties caused by enclosure of the common were likely to be felt most acutely by the *very* small owner, one of less than 10 acres, who lacked the resources to rent additional pasture and, moreover, lacked the means of meeting his enclosure and fencing costs without selling part, or all, of his already very small holding. It was to overcome the very small man's plight, no doubt, that in one unusual case, at Raunds in Northamptonshire in 1793, small owners with allotments of less than 10 acres each and 'in needy circumstances' had their costs and fencing paid for them by the large proprietors.[26] Very small owners, who were also very small farmers renting no additional land – really smallholders – and with very limited resources ('in needy circumstances' as Young's report had it), were probably those most severely hit by enclosure costs, even though their share of the costs might be almost negligible. Furthermore, their costs of ring-fencing were disproportionately heavy since the cost per acre rose the smaller the area to be fenced. Thus, in the early nineteenth century the cost of ring-fencing an allotment of 10 acres would be about £90 (without deductions for using existing fences or shared boundaries), while one of 5 acres was about £60, and one of 2.5 acres £40.

A little owner awarded, say, a 3-acre allotment in the early nineteenth century might have to pay only some £6 for his share of the public costs but another £40–50 for ring-fencing (not allowing for

---

25. Arthur Young, *General View of Norfolk*, 1804, p. 135.
26. Arthur Young, *Annals of Agriculture*, XLIV, 1806, p. 288.

possible savings by shared boundaries or using existing fences). His total bill, therefore, might be of the order of £30–60, while his land before enclosure could be worth about £30–40, and after enclosure £60. If he did not sell, he could have to pay (perhaps by borrowing) about as much as his land was worth, while he might not have sufficient credit with his neighbours to borrow that much. If unable, or unwilling, to borrow, his best option would be to sell before enclosure and take his £40, for with that he could rent and stock substantially more than 3 acres as a tenant, perhaps three or four times as much. This may well have been the most likely outcome for the very small owners whose sole asset was their little piece of land. Of course, this analysis is couched in 'worst case' terms, and often a very small owner might have been able to get through the enclosure without selling his land. But where he had to sell, or chose to sell, there were removal and disturbance expenses, and in numbers of instances the pain and regret of having to give up land that perhaps had been in the family for generations. This, to the very small owner, was the true cost of enclosure.

The difference in situation between small owner-occupiers and larger ones helps to explain why, very often, it was the small men and the commoners who opposed enclosure, while the bigger men, with more interest in farming for the market, and with superior powers of borrowing, not infrequently supported it.[27] The old communal system kept many small men in being, but with the prop of the common removed, numbers must have found it very difficult, and in some instances impossible, to survive.

The above discussion places the emphasis on *very small* owners, proprietors of only an acre or two, or former common right owners who were awarded a similar amount of land, or less, in an enclosure. Some of these owners chose, or were obliged, to sell as a result of the enclosure. Turner, in an important study of 1975, found, however, that there was a much more general dealing in land in the course of the Buckinghamshire enclosures he examined. While the total number of owners might not fall (or might even increase in some parishes), a substantial proportion – 30 per cent – of the owners having land before an enclosure had sold and left the parish in the course of a period of years stretching from soon before, to soon after, the event. The occasion of the enclosure certainly created an active market, especially in small parcels of land, and

27. Martin, 'Parliamentary Enclosure Movement', p. 27. In Warwickshire Martin found that freeholders supported enclosures in the period between 1742 and 1774.

Professor Turner believes that a large number of those selling did so in order to meet, or to avoid having to meet, the enclosure costs. The purchasers were either other small proprietors or those seeking to amalgamate small parcels into larger holdings. A number were local tradesmen or solicitors, as Dr Chapman found in the purchasers of land sold by the Commissioners in Hampshire. These purchasers might keep the former owners on the land as tenants[28] – a development which suggests the operation of a speculative element in the purchases, with tradesmen and buyers from outside the parish looking to make safe investments which, in time, might well rise in value or form the nucleus of a landed estate.

Turner's study, although based in part on land tax records, avoids most of the problems which we now know to bedevil this source of information about small owners. This is not the place to examine the pitfalls of the land tax, which has been very well done for us in Professor Donald Ginter's monumental study of 1992.[29] However, the essence of Ginter's findings is that land tax records cannot be used to analyse with any degree of accuracy the changes in numbers of small owners in various acreage categories; earlier studies which attempted to do this must be regarded as unreliable in detail.

Apart from the technical problems of the land tax records themselves, there is the difficulty, already mentioned above, that a small owner might rent additional land, and in reality be a substantial farmer: this will not be evident from the land tax. And there is the related problem that the parish can be a misleading basis for any investigation into small owners (or indeed owners of any size) since they might own other land (and rent other land) outside the parish in question. Again, where various members of a farming family, father, sons, uncles, cousins and less close relations, occupied land within one parish or over neighbouring parishes, examination of their surviving records indicates that, quite naturally, they helped one another in their farming, for example by lending one another spare pasture, horses, stock, implements, seed or, indeed, cash. Each might individually be only a small farmer, but as a group they possessed much greater resources than the mere individual acreages would indicate. The parish boundary, and the individual owner, were the units respected by enclosure Acts, and have formed the

28. M.E. Turner, 'Parliamentary Enclosure and Landownership Change in Buckinghamshire', *Economic History Review*, 2nd ser., XXVIII, 1975, pp. 568–70, 572–4.
29. Donald E. Ginter, *A Measure of Wealth: the English Land Tax in Historical Analysis*, Montreal, 1992.

basis of studies by modern investigators; farmers, however, knew no such limitation.

Historians have long supposed a secular decline in the numbers of small owners to have occurred in the course of the eighteenth century, and certainly their numbers were small in some areas on the eve of the French Wars. How far enclosure was responsible for a major part of a decline is uncertain, and other factors operating in the land market from early in the century may well have been more influential. Turner's Buckinghamshire study points to a considerable *turnover* of small owners but not to a large overall *decline*. Other studies, such as those of Dr J. M. Martin in Warwickshire, have pointed to the significance of location and period. In that county small owners did not always decline as a result of enclosure, and much depended on the farming environment and the period in question.[30] Even broader distinctions, having little or nothing to do with enclosure, have been emphasised by Professor John Beckett. Evidence from Cumbria, he found, indicated that pastoral areas were less likely to see a decline, and if it occurred it was likely to be in the era after 1815.[31]

Any decline due to enclosure was, of course, bound to be concentrated in the Midlands, where the parliamentary enclosures themselves were concentrated, where waste land was scarce and where the main object was usually to abolish the surviving open fields and commons. The loss of commons was probably the most widely felt disadvantage of enclosure for small owners, while the costs, especially those of fencing, often made very small holdings uneconomic. We should expect these factors alone to cause the sale of many small parcels of land, although of course the reasons for selling might be much more diverse: small owners sold because they were elderly or infirm and had no heir who could use the land; or because the capital was the key to setting up a different kind of business, or to renting farm land, or to obtaining an apprenticeship for a son or marrying off a daughter. We do not have to suppose that all the reasons for selling originated in the enclosure – rather, the enclosure, by stimulating the local land market, was the occasion for selling, providing the opportunity which was looked for, and giving impulse to motives which had long been present.

30. Martin, 'Parliamentary Enclosure Movement', p. 39.
31. J.V. Beckett, 'The Decline of the Small Landowner in Eighteenth Century and Nineteenth Century England: Some Regional Considerations', *Agricultural History Review*, XXX, 1982, pp. 109–10.

The opportunities of the land market activated by enclosure also stimulated sales by absentee owners, persons who had held small freeholds for some time, acquired perhaps through an old investment or through inheritance. Absentee owners, often living at distance, might have little personal or sentimental attachment to a certain piece of land, and the enclosure, when land values rose and much land was changing hands, was a clear inducement to sell. Some of the purchasers, as we have seen, did not become new owner-occupiers but rather new absentee owners, buying in order to add to an existing property, or merely as a small investment, a speculation that could prove profitable with small freeholds suitable as building sites or pleasure grounds.

At this distance in time it is impossible to be categorical about the changes in ownership which flowed from an enclosure. Some of them, no doubt, were involuntary, the effect of the costs or of the farming changes arising from the enclosure; but others were the consequence of the fillip which which was given to the local market in land – and indeed the changes in ownership were sometimes so numerous and prolonged as to long delay the efforts of the Commissioners to bring their business to a conclusion. There were both casualties of progress and beneficiaries: a balance is impossible to strike.

CHAPTER SEVEN

Parliamentary Enclosure and the Cottager

> But times are alter'd; trade's unfeeling train
> Usurp the land and dispossess the swain;
> Along the lawn, where scatter'd hamlets rose,
> Unwieldy wealth, and cumbrous pomp repose
> Oliver Goldsmith, *The Deserted Village* (1770)

When Goldsmith was writing his celebrated poem – only four years before his early death in 1774 – the pace of economic life was quickening. Trade was expanding, population growing, towns swelling, and industry spreading and adopting novel forms of production. And agriculture, too, was gradually changing in its organisation and technology. The enclosure of open fields and commons was a part of that change, and was often enough a preliminary to it. However, Goldsmith's poem appeared very early in the history of parliamentary enclosure, when the full flood of new Acts, over ninety a year in the early 1800s, was still a generation away. Wrote Goldsmith:

> Ill fares the land, to hastening ills a prey,
> When wealth accumulates, and men decay:
> Princes and lords may flourish or may fade;
> A breath can make them, as a breath has made;
> But a bold peasantry, the country's pride,
> When once destroy'd, can never be supplied.

Research of over twenty years ago has shown that, in fact, Goldsmith was not attacking the effects of parliamentary enclosures in general, but rather a separate and somewhat unusual phenomenon, the removal of villages to make way for the new seats and parks of large landowners. He had in mind one particular village near Oxford, which in 1761 he had seen removed by Lord Harcourt to make way for his new Palladian mansion and classical temple of a

124

church. Harcourt, who was not in some ways an unfeeling landlord, actually rebuilt the village, Nuneham Courtenay, as two lines of model red-brick and timber cottages on the main road leading from London to Oxford.[1]

The pulling down of old villages by landlords for the greater convenience of making parks was not very common in the eighteenth century, and where it occurred it was not usually connected with enclosure of open fields and commons, certainly not with parliamentary enclosure. Powerful landlords did encroach, both legally and illegally, on royal forests and wastes to enlarge their parks, and where necessary they bought up cottages and smallholdings for the purpose. Where a village was destroyed it was occasionally rebuilt on a new and less obtrusive site. This was of course an unpleasant manifestation of overbearing local power and wealth, and Goldsmith was voicing a justified hostility to this kind of destruction. The hostility was associated with a nostalgia for a remembered more placid past, a nostalgia which was to cling to the wider history of rural change for many decades to come. It is interesting, however, that Goldsmith's view of the matter was challenged at the time by William Whitehead, the poet laureate (who was, however, a close friend of the Harcourts), and also by the less prominent Revd Thomas Comber, an admirer of Arthur Young. The parson described Goldsmith as 'a dupe to vulgar prejudice', and doubted the accuracy of that line in his poem which stated that 'every rood of ground maintained its man'; he wished that 'a descriptive genius, like Dr Goldsmith' could have given 'the reverse of the medal. A picture of an *improved*, a cultivated country, would shine in the registry of Miltonics.'[2] Thus, early in the history of enclosure, although rural changes engendered hostility among the conservative, there were nevertheless those who recognised that the effects of enclosure could be beneficial for agricultural production, the supply of food and the creation of employment.

Enclosure of the commons

Much more important to most cottagers than the unlikely chance that their ancient homes might be pulled down, and new ones provided nearby, was the enclosure of the commons, a normal

1. Gillian Darley, *Villages of Vision*, 1975, pp. 6–8.
2. Thomas Comber, *A Free and Candid Correspondence on the Farmer's Letters . . . with the author Arthur Young, Esq.*, 1770, pp. 103–7.

accompaniment to parliamentary enclosure. The rights to use the common for pasture, for obtaining fuel, and for gathering wild berries and herbs, as well as for recreation and other purposes, was in many cases, if not all, valuable property that had to be compensated by Commissioners when the common was enclosed.

In his *Rural Economy of Yorkshire* of 1788 William Marshall, a leading agricultural authority of the time, set out his understanding of how common rights had become established and had developed.[3] Since access to the commons was from early times essential for the working of the open fields, 'every house which occupied a portion of the arable and meadow land of the township, had a right to a like portion of the herbage of the common pastures'.[4] Over the years it had gradually become a custom, which had since hardened into law, that no modern houses, 'nor even the lands of the township which lay to them, should enjoy either the fuel or the herbage of the commons'.[5] It is thus very clear that not every householder or cottager could legally claim a right to graze animals on the commons, even if in practice many persons without legal rights were permitted to do so. It followed also that a house without land had no right to the herbage of the commons.[6] It was generally understood, Marshall continued, and was considered as common law, 'that each common-right house has a power to summer as much stock on the commons as the lands which lie to it will winter'; or, in practice, a right to stock the commons in proportion to the value of the lands held with the common-right houses.[7]

By reference to ancient statutes, he went on, it might be inferred that the wood of a common belonged to the lord of the manor, except where a right of fuel, and of pannage (the feeding of swine on mast or the fruit of forest trees), had been established by long custom in favour of the holders of common rights.[8] Lastly, the right of cutting heath and peat for fuel went with the herbage of the common: the interest in the commons of lords of manors was confined to minerals, quarries and wood.[9]

The value of a common right, therefore, depended on the value of what the common produced by way of pasture, and in fuel and pannage, where custom allowed these to be taken. Enclosure Commissioners were bound to give due compensation to the *legal owners* of the houses and lands to which common rights were attached:

---

3. William Marshall, *The Rural Economy of Yorkshire*, I, York, 1788, pp. 61–7, 75–6.
4. Ibid., pp. 61–2.   5. Ibid., p. 63.   6. Ibid., p. 64.   7. Ibid., p. 67.
8. Ibid., p. 75.   9. Ibid., pp. 75–6.

this meant, of course, that they could not offer compensation to those persons who were merely the *tenants* of such houses and lands, who often actually exercised the rights to use the commons. There was no question of not compensating those who could prove a legal right, but Commissioners were often faced with claims of doubtful validity, claims which might well be disputed by other persons in the parish. To resolve such issues the Commissioners resorted to a variety of tests. A usual one was to ascertain whether the claimant had sufficient land to keep stock over winter. If he had not, then the claim failed because, as Marshall argued, a right to put stock on the commons in summer pre-supposed the means of keeping such stock in winter. Where a claimant based his right not on legal grounds but on long usage or suffrance, the Commissioners questioned the oldest inhabitants to ascertain whether, so long as they could remember (for 'time out of mind'), the claimant, or his family, had made use of the common without being challenged and fined by the legitimate common-right holders. And where a common-right house had been pulled down or destroyed by fire, the Commissioners generally followed Marshall in ruling that the common right had not been extinguished but was merely in suspense, to be revived when a new house was built on the site.

The rule of granting compensation to owners only, and not to tenants, was not invariably followed but was generally so. At Shefford in Bedfordshire, for example, the allotments made in compensation for the former common of 70 acres were given to the owners of the common rights, and the 'many cottagers' who formerly kept cows on the common were 'left without either stock or land'. These poor cottagers, we are told, had managed their cows in winter as best they could, 'a few sold them before winter, others bought food' for them.[10] At Eaton in the same county the twenty or so cottagers having rights were given allotments but kept fewer cows after the enclosure of 1796; however, many of them had not kept cows formerly. The persons most affected by the enclosure of the commons at Eaton were local higglers, petty traders in fish, gingerbread or apples, and who went in for carting for hire: they had previously turned their horses out on the commons without any right to do so, and afterwards were obliged to hire land for pasturing their animals.[11]

10. Arthur Young, 'Minutes Concerning Parliamentary Inclosures in the County of Bedford', *Annals of Agriculture*, XLII, 1804, p. 27.
11. Ibid., p. 39.

At Sayham and Ovington in Norfolk, enclosed in 1800, the owners of the hundred cottages with rights came out rather well: each was allotted 4 acres, and the value of a cottage with its new allotment rose to as much as £160. Moreover, every man who proved to the Commissioners' satisfaction that he had merely been in the habit of keeping stock on the common was considered as possessing a right and received an allotment in lieu. But at Shouldham and Garboise in the same county, the allotments made by the Commissioners for fuel were not equivalent to the plentiful supplies previously available from the commons. The cottagers' great complaint, however, was the loss of their livestock: they used to keep cows, mares, geese and ducks, but afterwards nothing – 'their language is . . . that they are ruined'. Numerous poor cottagers previously kept cows without having a common right and paid a small fine as an acknowledgement; they were not included in the allotments made as compensation, which were laid to the farms. Some sixty cows were kept before; afterwards none.[12]

Having decided who was to receive compensation for common rights, the Commissioners had next to decide the value to be placed upon the rights. This involved, as Marshall stipulated, a judgment of the value of the herbage, and of the fuel and pannage, where there were rights to these benefits. Where the common was stinted or regulated, that is, its pasture was limited to grazing by certain numbers and kinds of stock, and only for certain limited periods of the year – rules designed to prevent the common from being eaten bare – these limitations had to be taken into account. At Heacham in Norfolk, for instance, the fifty-five common-right houses belonged not to poor cottagers but to better-off tradesmen and small occupiers. The really poor, we are told, kept no stock other than geese, and had no right to gather fuel. The common rights were not very valuable, being confined to the feeding of two head of large cattle per right, and the Commissioners made compensation by an allotment of 2 acres of middling land or 1.5 acres of good quality for each right. There were at Heacham some twelve or fifteen small 'and very comfortable proprietors and renters of small plots, from two to 10 acres; who have cows and some corn, and what they like to cultivate'.[13] Also in Norfolk, in the large fenland parish of Northwold, the seventy-two common-right holders each received allotments supposed to be worth £8 10s a year, and with the allotments

12. Arthur Young, *General View of Norfolk*, 1804, pp. 156, 161.
13. Ibid., p. 125.

the value of a house rose three-fold after the enclosure to the high figure of £340. This was despite the fact that the allotments consisted partly of a piece of fen of between 4 and 6 acres, situated near the village but having the great drawback of being subject to inundations, while the remainder was made up of high fen, as much as four and a half miles from the village. The allotment proved, however, to be a hardship to the former common-right holders:

> the lands which would have suited them have been allotted to the great proprietors; all they can do is to mow it; thus in the winter they have no dry land on which to put their cattle. The allotments of fen ground for fuel, to common-rights, cannot be separated from the houses, neither let not sold from them, by a clause in the act of parliament.

The fuel allotment was 1.75 acres at Northwold, supposed to produce 12,000 turves a year, the calculated consumption of one hearth. Cottagers of twenty years' standing who had no common rights were treated meanly, being awarded permission only to cut up to 800 turves each a year – quite insufficient to keep a hearth alight – and this was made subject to the control of the fen reeves. A score of cottagers who had no common rights formerly kept 'half-starved cattle, geese, etc.', for which they were liable to be fined. 'These are all at an end; and the loss is not what might be supposed, for they were not profitable speculations by any means.'[14]

The harsh treatment that might be meted out to those without legitimate common rights perhaps more often arose from the inflexible attitudes of the landowners and farmers than from a lack of charity on the part of the Commissioners. It was an age of high respect for property, and usually a strict line was drawn between those who could legitimately prove a common right and those who could not. The legitimate proprietors were often hostile, for example, towards giving any compensation for illegal encroachments on the commons, even though the encroachments might be extremely numerous and very old-established. Kingsclere common in Hampshire, for instance, was subject to as many as eighty encroachments, stretching from merely 'a small part of a Garden' to as much as 'a neat Cottage with Stable, piggery and Garden, well fenced in'. At the Hawley enclosure of 1815–19 in the same county the Commissioners agreed – whether willingly or not is not clear – to the view put forward by the landowners that allotments should not be given to those claiming for encroachments of less than fifty years' standing,

14. Ibid., pp. 147–8.

even though a rent or other acknowledgement had never been demanded for the encroachments in the past.[15] And in Elvetham, enclosed in 1813, the cottages on the common of less than twenty years' standing were left unrecognised and were awarded to the freeholder or to the lord of the manor: only the cottages of longer standing were to become the property of the occupiers, and then only if a rent had been paid to the lord of the manor.[16]

The allotment of land made in compensation for a common right was often very small in quantity. In *The Village Labourer*, J.L. and Barbara Hammond refer to some very tiny allotments ranging between 12 perches (363 square yards, less than one-thirteenth of an acre) and 1.5 acres. They make the point that such small parcels were of little use to cottagers and, moreover, were expensive to fence.[17] Indeed, unless thrown together and worked cooperatively, they were too small for anything but a few poultry, vegetables, soft fruit, or for making little orchards. They were by no means equivalent to having the whole run of a large common for keeping a cow, and perhaps extensive numbers of geese and ducks. It is also true that the Commissioners did not always compensate common-right holders with land suited to their purposes, as was seen in the case of Northwold. Another example of this failing occurred at Sandy in Bedfordshire. This was a parish abounding with market gardeners, of whom no fewer than sixty-three were proprietors at the time of enclosure. These men

> kept cows on the boggy common, and cut fern for litter on the warren, by which means they were enabled to raise manure for their gardens besides fuel in plenty: the small allotments of an acre and a half, however good the land, has been no compensation for what they were deprived of.
>
> They complain heavily, and know not how they will now manage to raise manure. This was no reason to preserve the deserts in their old state, but an ample one for giving full compensation.[18]

It is likely that very often the smallness of the allotments given in lieu of common rights reflected the fact that the common before enclosure was of limited value, rather than any general wish on the part of the Commissioners to defraud common-right owners. These included, it should be remembered, as well as small occupiers and

---

15. Hants. RO: 11M 49/465; 50M 63 Box 4.   16. Hants. RO: 50M 63 Box 1.
17. J.L. and Barbara Hammond, *The Village Labourer*, 1978 edn, p. 61.
18. Report by Arthur Young in Thomas Batchelor, *General View of Bedfordshire*, 1808, p. 240.

cottagers, a number of substantial proprietors who were quite capable of asserting their interests. In some parishes, even where the rights were numerous, few were owned by genuine cottagers.[19] A common right was frequently valued at worth only a few pounds per annum, and so an allotment of land in lieu was a small area of land that, if let, would produce the same income. For example, at Lidlington (Beds.), enclosed in 1775, the common rights were valued at £2 2s per annum each. The average annual value of the field land there was about 14s per acre, and consequently the allotments given in lieu were each of 3 acres.[20] Where the right was valued at a lower figure, perhaps considerably lower, and the average value of the land was high, then of course quite small allotments would result. Certainly a very small allotment was insufficient for keeping a cow, but there is plenty of evidence that cottagers frequently pooled their allotments and worked them jointly. Even where, for the occupiers' convenience, the allotments were laid out adjoining the cottages, a cooperative system of cultivation was often followed. In the era of high grain prices during the Napoleonic Wars the cottagers often preferred to grow corn rather than keep cows, as happened for instance at Carlton and Weston Colville in Cambridgeshire.[21]

Of course, those people who used to keep cows and could no longer do so when the common was enclosed had a serious grievance and felt themselves robbed of a valuable asset. Visiting Maulden in Bedfordshire after its enclosure, Arthur Young was told by a farmer and some cottagers that 'enclosing would ruin England; it was worse than ten wars'. 'Why, my friend, what have you lost by it?', Young asked. 'I kept four cows before the parish was enclosed and now I don't keep so much as a goose, and you ask me what I lose by it!' This was an enclosure which occasioned much rioting, as Young noted, and soldiers had to be sent from Coventry to quell the disturbances.[22]

A cow, together perhaps with some poultry and pigs, was a valuable contribution to the economy of cottage households, and apart from the important additions made to the larder, the occasional sale of a calf, a mature pig or a goose helped meet major outlays such as those for winter clothing and boots, repairs to the cottage, apprenticeship of the children, funerals, and loss of work due to

19. See Arthur Young, 'Minutes Concerning Parliamentary Inclosures in the County of Cambridge', *Annals of Agriculture*, XLIII, 1805, p. 43.
20. Young, 'Parliamentary Inclosures in the County of Bedford', p. 50.
21. Young, 'Parliamentary Inclosures in the County of Cambridge', pp. 114, 117.
22. Batchelor, *Bedfordshire*, p. 235.

illness or accidents. The lack of livestock was no doubt felt the more where the keeping of stock on the common was formerly permitted by tenancy of a common-right cottage or by payment of a small fine, rather than solely by the absolute possession of a right which received compensation on enclosure. On the other hand, it has to be remembered that not all cottagers made use of their common rights – indeed sometimes a right was let to a neighbour who wanted to keep more stock than a single right permitted: much depended on what means were available for keeping stock over winter.[23] Sometimes the cottagers were actually too poor to keep any stock whatsoever,[24] and if they could afford to have a cow they could not replace it when it died.

Opposition to enclosure was not infrequent. It took various forms from open protests, marches and public meetings to illegal outbursts like the removal of the surveyor's pegs, pulling down of fences and physical attacks on surveyors and Commissioners. Dr Neeson refers to numerous instances in her study of enclosure in Northamptonshire.[25] As we have seen, opposition appears to have been most hostile and prolonged where large numbers of people had access to the commons, and especially where extensive areas of marshland or upland waste were to be enclosed, affecting a number of parishes and leaving numerous small farmers and husbandmen without free grazing and cottagers without their former occupations of cow-keeping, fishing, wildfowling and cutting sedge.[26]

In Cardiganshire for example, the work of enclosing the moorlands was held up by mobs of hostile poor who might number as many as a hundred and fifty, and included women armed with dripping pans. The rioters threw down fences and attacked surveyors who were attempting to take measurements: one surveyor was knocked to the ground and had his chain and theodolite stolen. The cottagers feared the loss of their right to cut turf for fuel, even though large acreages were set aside by the Commissioners for this purpose.[27] The enclosure of upland moors in various parts of Wales was at its height during the Napoleonic Wars, when high food prices encouraged the cultivation of waste lands. But at the same time the loss of open moorland spread severe poverty among the

23. Young, 'Parliamentary Inclosures in the County of Cambridge', p. 45.
24. Ibid., p. 57.
25. J.M. Neeson, *Commoners: Common Right, Enclosure and Social Change in England, 1700–1820*, Cambridge, 1993, ch. 9.
26. Chapter 3, pp. 51–3.
27. David J.V. Jones, 'Distress and Discontent in Cardiganshire 1814–19', *Ceredigion*, V, 1966, pp. 280, 282–6.

population. Dispossession of squatters who had encroached on the commons was one cause of the unrest, in which landowners were attacked, and in one incident a mob, two hundred strong, marched to Flint gaol and rescued a labourer who had been charged with pulling down fences. In 1812 in the Llŷn peninsula a group of women bombarded the Commissioner, his clerk and the surveyor with sods of earth and forced them to retreat. Magistrates and their constables were subsequently attacked and prevented from executing warrants for arrest, while some miles away the surveyors had to be protected by a party of dragoons. Some of the rioters were caught, however, and two of the ringleaders sentenced to death, a sentence commuted in one case to imprisonment; two prominent female rioters were given six months each.[28]

It is clear that when large areas of widely used common or fenland, marsh, moor and other extensive wastes were threatened by enclosure, the local inhabitants were very likely to protest. They included not only small farmers and the cottagers working on larger farms but also craftsmen and tradesmen, and often numbers of industrial workers who made use of the waste. This kind of land had always been open to local people wanting to graze stock, keep horses, take fish, rabbits and birds, and gather fuel for their hearths. The enclosures were regarded as depriving the poor of what had always been theirs, and claims to exclusive ownership put forward by wealthy landowners were rejected as unjust and treated with scorn. This is not to say that the enclosure of parishes that were mainly agricultural went off without difficulty. Small occupiers in a farming village were often apprehensive of the effects on their livelihood, and cottagers, local craftsmen and other workers there feared the loss of the advantages offered by the commons.

Not all commons were of much advantage, of course. Sometimes they were very small or severely stinted, or, through lack of regulation, eaten bare or covered with weeds. Indeed, an unstinted common was generally of very little advantage to the holders of the rights. At Ropsley in Lincolnshire, for example, the 'common cow pasture', so-called, was 'covered almost all over with Gorse and Thorns', and was used only for cutting gorse for fuel.[29] But, frequently, there was much to lose. In 1818 the cottagers of Pointon in Lincolnshire petitioned Earl Fortescue against having to exchange their existing common for allotments of 4 acres each of less good

28. David J.V. Jones, *Before Rebecca: Popular Protests in Wales 1793–1835*, 1973, pp. 41–8.
29. Lincs. RO: Cragg MSS 1/7/3.

land. Such a quantity would make it impossible, they said, to keep more than one cow, and they asked for enough land to keep two cows as formerly. The cows were important since, as they pointed out, the cottagers were often out of work for part of the year; moreover, several of them were too old and infirm to change their way of life.[30]

The possibility of incurring unpopularity, or of stirring up more active protest, was a consideration which made some local gentry and clergy wish to be excused from taking a prominent part in promoting an enclosure. Correspondence of 1777 regarding Goring in Oxfordshire provides an example of this. The Revd P.L. Powys, Prebendary of Bristol, told the landowner, John Nicholls, that he did not wish to be involved

> as I live constantly on the spot, and it must naturally be expected that I shall feel the effects of that discontent which things of this nature generally produce amongst the Cottagers and those who for various reasons may be inclined to oppose the scheme

In seeking to re-assure him, John Nicholls replied:

> most certainly a compensation must be made to the Cottagers for their right of Common, and if this is done honestly and liberally I cannot see why they should object to the Enclosure.

Twenty-four years later, in 1801, these same individuals were again in correspondence, this time over the enclosure of nearby Goring Heath. John Nicholls assured the Revd Powys that the enclosure would cost very little, although other objections had been raised:

> I have been told you were adverse to it from the idea that it would be a less pleasant hunting country – I am not a judge of this but it would probably be always left in large divisions as the Goring Common Field is. In respect of the Cottagers they would be benefited by an increased demand for their labour and as to any emoluments they now derive from it, I would readily concur in any measure which might secure them an equivalent. . . . The distress for corn lately experienced has convinced the nation at large of the necessity of bringing *waste* land into cultivation.[31]

The value of the commons

For many cottagers – those whom contemporaries described as 'the poor' (by no means always meant as a term of contempt) – the unenclosed commons played a significant part in their lives. The

---

30. Lincs. RO: Cragg MSS 1/8/2.   31. Oxon. RO: PL xiv/1, 3.

most valuable and most general advantage, the keeping of a cow, was worth in milk an average in 1798 of 3s 6d a week, or £9 2s a year – according to Nathaniel Kent, a prominent land agent and agricultural authority.[32] He set the profit to be made from the calf against the loss when the cow was dry, and allowed an average yield of only 6 quarts a day at a penny per quart. Three acres of good land, rented at 30s an acre, would be sufficient to keep a cow in good condition, he said, with one of the three acres to be divided off for mowing in order to provide hay for the winter. With tithes and parish rates the total outlay would be £5 4s, not allowing for the cottager's own labour. Further, the surplus milk would feed a pig, again a great means of adding to the cottager's income. If the cow were grazed on a reasonably well-regulated common, rather than on rented pasture, the profit would be even higher, of course. The return to be obtained from the cow was not trivial when compared with the wages then earned by a day labourer, which were some 9–12s a week, and only half as much for a wife who worked full-time, and even less for children.

The contrary view was advanced at the same time by another well-known agricultural expert, John Billingsley (who was engaged to report on the county of Somerset for the Board of Agriculture). Billingsley believed the commons to be of little benefit to cottagers. Those on moorlands were frequently subject to flooding, obliging the cottagers to rent other pasture for their cows, while the great majority of cottagers were short of winter keep because they did not rent land for that purpose. The more productive commons, he said, were monopolised by large farmers whose numerous stock kept the cottagers' beasts in a starved condition. The fact that a common right could be rented for as little as 10–12s a year revealed how little it was really worth, and, furthermore, 'in sauntering after his cattle' the cottager acquired 'a habit of indolence. . . . Day-labour becomes disgusting to him . . . and at length the sale of a half-fed calf, or hog, furnishes the means of adding intemperance to idleness.'[33]

The truth probably lies somewhere in the middle of these two extreme views. It is likely that rather few commons provided cottagers with really good pasture for their cows, if we may judge from the remarks of the contemporaries who saw them; equally, few commons were of little or no value, though certainly some fell into this

32. Nathaniel Kent, 'The Great Advantage of a Cow to the Family of a Labouring Man', *Annals of Agriculture*, XXXI, 1798, p. 22.
33. John Billingsley, 'Uselessness of Commons to the Poor', *Annals of Agriculture*, XXXI, 1798, pp. 28–31.

category. So far from leading cottagers into idleness, Young gathered evidence which suggested that ownership of a little property, be it only a single cow, gave a man a feeling of independence in which he could take pride, a pride sufficient to keep him from looking to the parish for support from the poor rates.[34] He collected numerous examples where the enclosure of the commons had resulted in fewer cows being kept and consequently the poor had suffered, though there were others where they had been treated well and had benefited.[35] Many allotments awarded to common-right holders were considerably smaller than the 2 to 4 acres which opinion held were necessary for maintaining a cow. In this respect much depended on the quality of the soil (although William Cobbett in his *Cottage Economy* described how it was possible to maintain a cow on as little as 40 rods, that is, a quarter of an acre[36]).

In any case, a major difficulty, as we have seen, was that the compensation for common rights was made to the *owners* (who included the farmers and some smallholders, as well, usually, as numbers of cottagers). Those cottagers who used the commons as *occupiers*, rather than as owners, or merely *by custom*, usually received nothing by way of compensation and so had to give up their cows. Sometimes the enclosure Act specified that land was to be set aside and vested in trustees to produce funds to be spent on fuel for the poor; but except where interested landowners, like the Earl of Winchelsea, insisted on the Commissioners setting land aside for cow pastures, this kind of provision was seldom made. One interesting exception, however, is found in the Act for Cobham, Surrey, which was enclosed in 1793. The Act allowed for 300 acres to be left as common, scattered about the parish in various pieces for the convenience of the cottagers. Use of this land was confined to those less well-off persons not occupying houses with land worth more than £10 a year, and about seventy cottagers so entitled were registered in the Award. It was reported that few of them had in fact kept cows before the enclosure: the great advantage of the newly provided common land was for fuel and keeping geese; the pasture was said to be far better than formerly because now the farmers were excluded from access to it.[37]

---

34. Arthur Young, 'An Inquiry into the Propriety of Applying Wastes to the Better Maintenance and Support of the Poor', *Annals of Agriculture*, XXXVI, 1801, pp. 502, 581.

35. Ibid., pp. 513–15.   36. William Cobbett, *Cottage Economy*, 1912 edn, p. 81.

37. Arthur Young, 'Minutes of Inclosures', *Annals of Agriculture*, XLV, 1806, pp. 304–5.

Of course, the commons and waste lands were never free from disputes and grievances, even before enclosure. There were certainly parishes, like Conington in Cambridgeshire, where all the common rights were in the hands of the farmers and the parson, and the poor had no rights at all.[38] Or ones like Cheshunt in Hertfordshire, where the common, a very large one of over 1,100 acres, was in the hands of 'a parcel of jobbers', meaning men who hired out horses; the jobbers had rented the common-right cottages so as to have exclusive use of the pasture and the cottagers themselves had no right of access.[39] Encroachments on the waste made by large landowners caused as much of a grievance to cottagers as their encroachments, and those of squatters, did to lords of manors. The waste, like many commons, was subject to competing claims between landowners and customary users, and some disputes rumbled on for years before brought to an end by enclosure.[40]

Nevertheless, access to an unenclosed common, even if disputed, was better than having no common at all. Those who did not possess the common rights knew that, on enclosure, no allotments would go to them, and so far as they were concerned 'cow-keeping amongst the poor will be at an end'. At Guilden Morden in Cambridgeshire, Young reported,

> the alarm among them is very great; they hold the idea of an inclosure and the preparatory steps taken with a sort of terror; they know well the fact that they must suffer, and dread it accordingly. When an evil could be so easily prevented, and inclosure converted to their advantage as well as to that of every other class, it is to be lamented that measures are not taken with this view.[41]

It was true that enclosure was often followed by a great increase in employment, a big advantage when the cottager class was expanding with the growth of the rural population as a whole. Employment increased particularly where pasture, and especially poor waste-land pasture, was converted to arable. An example of this comes from the fenland parish of March, Cambridgeshire, enclosed in 1793. The 1,500 acres of higher land not subject to flooding were converted to tillage, including part of the commons which had formerly been 'much overrun with rushes, thistles etc.'. There were 180 common

---

38. Young, 'Parliamentary Inclosures in Cambridgeshire', *Annals of Agriculture*, XLII, 1804, p. 506.
39. Arthur Young, *General View of Hertfordshire*, 1804, p. 45.
40. Graham Rogers, 'Custom and Common Right: Waste Land Enclosure and Social Change in West Lancashire', *Agricultural History Review*, XLI, 1993, pp. 146–9.
41. Young, 'Parliamentary Inclosures in Cambridgeshire', p. 497.

rights, but the commons were so extensive that a single right
provided access for a substantial number of beasts, and the rights
were made the more valuable by each having 9 acres of mowing
ground for hay; after the enclosure the letting value of a common
right rose from an unusually high £7 a year to as much as £20. While
those persons without common rights had after the enclosure more
opportunity of finding employment, there were some twenty families who before made a living from keeping dairy cows but were
now reduced to seeking day labour or obliged to emigrate.[42]

The fate of the dairymen at March reminds us that many of
those who suffered from the enclosure of commons were not
cottagers but small farmers, whose business depended crucially on
the availability of free or cheap pasture. A similar story was told at
Barton Mills in Suffolk, where the commons consisted of some 300
acres of fen and 500 of sheepwalk out of a total of 1,900 acres in
the parish. 'The poor', it was reported, did not lose by the enclosure, but others did, very severely. These included 'little owners of
£20, or £30, or £40 a year', some of whom kept seven, eight or ten
cows on the commons in the summer, and wintered them on the
straw of their 15 or 20 acres of arable. After the enclosure they
found themselves with allotments of 20 or 25 acres in lieu of their
common rights – good land, but not enough of it to feed a team
of horses nor half the cows they kept before. 'They were forced to
sell immediately.'[43]

Indeed, there must have been many instances where the principal losers by enclosure of the commons were not cottagers, many
of whom always relied on farm work for a part of their income, but
dairymen, market-gardeners, poultry-keepers and other small producers who once enjoyed a large degree of independence. The
additional employment often created by enclosure offered some
mitigation of their plight, as it did for the cottagers; but it did not
compensate for the loss of independence or the old pride in possession, nor yet for the degradation in status to that of a farmer's
cowman or, worse, day-labourer.

Fortunately, in numerous districts there were alternatives available. Many of the cottagers did not in fact work on the land but had
full-time employment as blacksmiths, wheelwrights, mill-wrights, carpenters, joiners, bricklayers and glaziers, or as weavers, shoemakers
or framework-knitters in the hosiery trade. Professor E.A. Wrigley

42. Ibid., p. 323.   43. Arthur Young, *General View of Suffolk*, 1813, pp. 43–4.

has shown that, in rural counties alone, employment in the ten trades of baker, blacksmith, bricklayer, butcher, carpenter, mason, publican, shoemaker, shopkeeper and tailor increased from 134,189 to 164,418 in the twenty years before 1851; in the rest of England it rose from 382,790 to 555,907.[44] And no doubt these ten trades, as well as others had been on the increase in earlier decades when the parliamentary enclosures were at their height.

Some small farmers and cottagers had always combined a little piece of arable and some sheep or cows with a part-time craft, or with innkeeping, higgling or petty trading, a carrier's business or dealing in coal or logs. When times were slack in their craft or trade they concentrated more on the land and their livestock; when trade was brisk they neglected their land and perhaps gave it up altogether. Frequently, the cottager's wife and children looked after the cows, pigs and poultry, while he spent the whole day at his main occupation.

In the period of enclosure that occupation might well be overtaken by new techniques, as textiles and much of iron-working and machine-making moved into factories or large works; but at the same time flour mills, bone mills, corn and meal warehouses, tanyards and leather-dressing shops all increased, and there was a growth also in brickworks, paper mills and cement works, to say nothing of breweries, gas- and water-works, town dairies and bakeries, coal merchants and a wide variety of town shops. As towns and suburbs expanded there was a mounting demand for men who could drive carriages, carts and wagons, repair the roads, and look after horses, stables and gardens. The huge growth in horse-drawn traffic, in both towns and countryside, greatly augmented the opportunities for men who wanted to continue working in the open air rather than in a confined workshop, and who had experience of driving hoses and looking after animals. Clearly, it must not be supposed that when men sought alternatives to life on the land their only option was to enter a factory in a large industrial town. There were many other possibilities open to them nearer to hand in towns large and small as well as in large villages.

When the commons were enclosed the women and children were often left without livestock to care for. But in many parts of

44. E.A. Wrigley, 'Men on the Land and Men in the Countryside: Employment in Agriculture in Early Nineteenth-Century England', in Lloyd Bonfield, Richard M. Smith and Keith Wrightson, eds, *The World We have Gained: Histories of Population and Social Structure*, Oxford, 1986, p. 300.

the country other occupations sprang up or became more wide-spread. Workshops and small factories, employing mainly women, developed in country towns and villages, particularly in textiles, hosiery, boots and shoes, and in specialities such as making pickles and preserves. And hand trades also flourished. Among them were the making of gloves in Oxfordshire and parts of the West Country; string, cordage, nets, sailcloth and sacking in Dorset; pillow lace in north Bedfordshire, Buckinghamshire and Northamptonshire; and straw plaiting in Buckinghamshire, south Bedfordshire, Suffolk and Hertfordshire. The rise of straw plaiting in the last county, mainly for making hats and bonnets, was chronicled in the Board of Agriculture's county *Report* of 1804. Round Stevenage, Hatfield and Redbourn, and also at St Albans, Berkhamsted and Hitchin, straw plaiting had replaced the dying craft of spinning as the occupation of women and girls. The earnings were high: women could earn a pound a week at it, and girls as much as 15s, quite comparable with what men could get on the farms. So high were the earnings that the farmers complained 'it makes the poor saucy, and no servants can be found, or any field-work done, where this manufacture establishes itself'.[45]

Of course, new and profitable occupations did not appear every-where, and many women and girls who needed paid work found it as they had always done, in domestic service. As the number of better-off families grew, in both country and town, so the demand for servants grew also; and it has to be remembered that even very modest households, such as those of master craftsmen, shop-keepers and clerks, could often find room and money for at least one servant, as a glance at Dickens will confirm. Fewer men and boys than females were employed as servants, and those mainly in stables and gardens, but as we have seen there were many other openings for them in the busier towns and villages. Domestic serv-ice was an enormous outlet for labour, both skilled and unskilled, ranging from housekeepers and governesses to house and kitchen maids, and from butlers and coachmen to stable lads. The Census of 1841 showed that domestic service was indeed the country's second largest occupational group, and included 255,000 males and 989,000 females, a total of 1,244,000. This may be compared with agricultural employment, which in 1831 occupied nearly 981,000 males over 30 alone.

45. Young, *Hertfordshire*, pp. 222–4.

Villages varied greatly in the numbers of servant-employing house-holds they contained. Some had many more gentry and middle-class families, or well-to-do tradesmen and craftsmen, than others. But it may not be unfair to take as an example of a better-off com-munity the large village of Welwyn in Hertfordshire. Its population in 1851 numbered 1,557, and at that date it had eight farmers who employed between them sixty-six men and eight boys, while another fifty-three farm-workers were listed in the Census. There were also, among others, two blacksmiths, a wheelwright, a miller, a saddler and harness-maker, a cattle dealer, and also shoemakers, carpenters, grocers, butchers, bakers, tailors, linen drapers and coal merchants. Welwyn's families and its inns gave work to as many as 35 males and no fewer than 113 females: no small addition to the employment possibilities of the neighbourhood.[46]

Movement in the countryside, and to towns and villages offering greater employment opportunities, took place despite the hindrance of the Settlement Laws. These statutes were designed to establish local responsibility for providing relief to the poor, and to limit the burden of the poor rates upon an individual parish. Those persons most severely restricted to their home parish were probably those already on relief, and especially ones saddled with large families. However, the Justices were often willing to issue certificates which allowed the unemployed to seek work outside their own parish, and with or without certificates many people did in fact move, usually over short distances but quite often further afield. Research has indicated that areas with growing farm work and industry and trade where more labour was needed were able to draw freely on other districts of plentiful labour, revealing a more flexible pattern of movement than used to be thought.

It remains a controversial issue whether the records of settle-ment examinations, to ascertain among other things the parish responsible for relief, may be used as indicators of the extent and timing of unemployment. What is clear, however, is that people did move away from their home parishes to seek work or find better employment. Some migrants went not to large cities or country towns but to other villages, even those which had relatively little industry. The 1851 Census shows this to have been commonplace. The west Kent village of Otford, for example, had in that year so high

---

46. W. Branch Johnson, *Welwyn Briefly: Two Thousand years in Outline of a Hertford-shire village*, Welwyn, 1960, pp. 64–5.

a proportion as over 49 per cent of its inhabitants born outside the parish: 20 per cent came from nearby parishes, another 14 per cent from other parishes in Kent, and 15 per cent from outside the county.[47]

Enclosure and farm employment

While many alternative employments were expanding, what effect did enclosure have on employment on the farms? Clearly, where the common was enclosed and small occupiers and cottagers lost a valuable means of maintaining or supplementing their livelihood, they were forced either to seek some other occupation, perhaps elsewhere, or, in a more wholly agricultural parish, to rely on full-time work on farms. In this connection it is important to remember that, nationally, the *total numbers employed in agriculture were expanding*. Investigation of the Census figures for agricultural employment in the early nineteenth century shows that the expansion was much less than the Census totals suggest, and probably did not exceed a rise of some 11 per cent over the forty years between 1811 and 1851. Nevertheless, the numbers employed were growing, if at a modest rate compared with that of the population at large. There still lives on a persistent myth that because of the contemporary changes in farming, including enclosure, the opposite was occurring. This misconception probably arises from the fact that although employment in the agricultural sector was expanding, albeit at a slow rate, it was falling as a proportion of the rapidly rising total employment throughout the country. The recent evidence indicates, interestingly, that most of the increase in agricultural employment arose from a relatively rapid growth of small-scale production catering for the needs of the increasingly large cities and industrial areas.[48]

Of course, an overall rise in the total numbers is not inconsistent with some local declines in agricultural employment. Much depended on shifts in the geographical pattern of the rising demand

47. James Stephen Taylor, *Poverty, Migration and Settlement in the Industrial Revolution: Sojourners' Narratives*, Palo Alto, Calif., 1989; K.D.M. Snell, *Annals of the Labouring Poor: Social Change and Agrarian England 1660–1900*, Cambridge, 1985; Norma Landau, 'The Laws of Settlement and the Surveillance of Migration in Eighteenth-Century Kent', *Continuity and Change*, 3, 1988, pp. 391–420; Norma Landau, 'The Regulation of Immigration, Economic Structures and Definitions of the Poor in Eighteenth Century England', *Historical Journal*, 33, 1990, pp. 541–72; Dennis Clarke and Anthony Stoyel, *Otford in Kent: a History*, Otford, Kent, 1975, p. 205.

48. Wrigley, 'Men on the Land', pp. 296, 315–18.

for farm products, as well as on how the nature of the farming was affected by the abolition of open fields and commons in that substantial fraction of the countryside affected by enclosure. This, in turn, depended on the nature of the soil and access to markets. In many parishes only a scrap of field land and commons was left to enclose, while in some others the fields had already ceased to be the basis of the farming. In these circumstances any effects were likely to be small. However, where large-scale enclosure was followed by an increase in permanent pasture at the expense of former arable, a decline in employment might follow; where the arable increased, on the other hand, or rotations which included grass leys or temporary pastures were adopted, the work available would be increased, since these types of farming occupied more hands on a given acreage than did permanent pasture.

Wherever the farming became more intensive it was certain to be more intensive in labour also. Cultivation of potatoes and other roots and vegetables had high labour requirements, though much of this labour was provided by women rather than men. The small-scale production that was expanding near centres of population to meet the growing demand for dairy products, market garden produce and poultry and fruit was particularly labour-intensive, each enterprise employing usually only one man and his family. And where much waste land was enclosed, moors reclaimed for cultivation and marshes drained, the increased demand for labour was likely to be great. Lastly, it should be remembered that parliamentary enclosure did not affect the whole country equally: only the central Midland counties were heavily enclosed, and as we saw in Chapter 2, there were many counties where little land was affected, and that largely waste, so adding to local employment.

It is very difficult to generalise about the effects of enclosure on agricultural employment. So much depended on changes in land use, as just seen, the adoption locally of more intensive cultivation, and the bringing into use of former uncultivated land. And these changes derived in turn from market demands and movements in prices. Taking these factors together, it seems unlikely that the employment effects, although often significant locally, would have been very large nationally, especially when it is remembered that parliamentary enclosure affected only about a quarter of the country.

During the period of parliamentary enclosure the market for agricultural produce was expanding very rapidly. Not only did the population rise from some 5.8 millions in 1751 to 8.7 millions in

1801 and to 13.3 millions by 1831 – an overall rise of nearly 130 per cent – but the non-agricultural proportion of that population, the proportion which had to be fed by those farming for the market (with, latterly, some help from food imports), rose from 54 per cent in 1750 to nearly 79 per cent by 1851.[49] In response to this tremendous growth in demand, estimates indicate that English agricultural output roughly doubled between 1750 and 1850.[50]

Part of the large increase in output and labour productivity resulted from the advantages of parliamentary enclosure: the freeing of occupiers to make the best use of their land, the removal of common rights and communal restrictions on enterprise, and the bringing into cultivation of former rough pastures, moors, heaths, marshes and other 'waste' lands. With the growth of the market there was some shift towards increased cultivation of crops, especially as grain prices soared during the French Wars; and, as we have noted, crop production required a larger labour force than pasture. But although some recently enclosed farmland, and especially waste land, saw an extension of cereal cultivation, other old arable land saw the opposite, a conversion to grass for dairying and fattening, the more especially in the neighbourhood of expanding towns with a growing local market for milk, butter, cheese and meat.

The issue is made the more complicated by the concurrent rise of industry – the growth of new factory industries and also the expansion of many old hand trades. Both of these developments occurred in country towns and villages, if at a later stage the major activity shifted more towards large industrial towns. Increasingly the inhabitants of the countryside became affected by the instability of industry, its periodical booms and slumps, as much as by the changes in agriculture. Even where there was no industrial growth, there were still other employment opportunities. The choice facing the young country man or woman was not confined to a simple one between the land or industry – if indeed industrial employment was available. The country town and large village had its various trades and crafts, as we have seen. And there was still the biggest field for female employment (as well as for many males), domestic service. The alternatives to leaving the land were not either an arduous, ill-paid factory job or the perils of emigration: they were remarkably numerous, at least for the young and able-bodied.

49. Mark Overton, *Agricultural Revolution in England*, Cambridge, 1996, pp. 75, 138.
50. Ibid., p. 75.

Let us return to the direct employment effects of enclosure on agricultural workers. Arthur Young, in his earlier years a staunch advocate of enclosure, had no doubt of the beneficial employment effects, at least where new fodder crops and improved types of cereal production followed. Consider, he said, 'the great numbers of men that . . . are constantly employed in hedging and ditching'; the effects of growing turnips 'hand-hoed twice, and then drawn by hand, and carted to the stalls for beasts' on land that formerly lay fallow; and the numerous other labour-intensive crops now more widely grown – beans and peas, potatoes, carrots, coleseed – which involved the use of more hands in their cultivation.[51] Young's argument was taken up and expanded by the modern historian Professor Chambers, in a well-known article of 1953.[52] Chambers added some further points, noting that where the soil was too heavy for turnips convertible grass leys served as an alternative, while in general the greater output of farming provided more work for rural trades and industries. In opposition to Marx, he concluded that 'the enclosure acts had the effects of further reducing, but not of destroying the remaining English peasantry'.[53]

A more recent observer, Crafts, has pointed out that enclosure was only one factor, and not the most important one, in the migration of labour.[54] This raises further complicated issues because of the variety of forces which influenced the generally high migration of the time of parliamentary enclosure, with men and women moving from the countryside to towns and other growing industrial centres. Again, for the period of the French Wars when enclosure was at its height, the problem is obscured by the shortages of farm labour caused by the accelerated expansion of industry and recruitment for the armed forces. The war period was marked by long runs of exceptionally bad seasons, acute shortages and high food prices. The price of wheat, now the staple for bread over much of the country, shot up from the 48–58 shillings per quarter level of the early 1790s, and in the worst years rose to fantastic heights, the average price for 1800 mounting to 113s 10d, and for 1801 to 119s 6d. Food riots broke out, directed in part at farmers, and had to be cowed by the military. The farmers were handicapped by shortages

51. Arthur Young, *Political Arithmetic*, 1774, pp. 72–3.
52. J.D. Chambers, 'Enclosure and Labour Supply in the Industrial Revolution', *Economic History Review*, 2nd ser., V, 1953, pp. 319–43.
53. Ibid., pp. 333–4, 335.
54. N.F.R. Crafts, 'Enclosure and Labour Supply Revisited', *Explorations in Economic History*, XV, 1978, pp. 45–7.

of labour as well as the badness of the seasons, and the labour problem had already appeared in some areas as early as 1796. A country gentleman writing from a village near Nottingham in September of that year referred to the scarcity of wheat and the poor harvest weather. But, he said, 'the great complaint of the farmers is the Tediousness of the Harvest, and the Scarcity of Labourers and the Extravagance of their Wages. Some farmers have been obliged to mow their Wheat for want of Reapers.'[55]

There is yet another contemporary issue which confuses the problem of enclosure and employment – poverty. Modern opinion sees the root cause of the growth of poverty at this time in the rapid increase in population. The numbers of the country's inhabitants grew by 50 per cent in the half-century after 1750, and by a further 93 per cent in the following half-century. Although industry and commerce were expanding, and employment in agriculture, domestic service and many other fields was growing also, the rising demand for work maintained a restrictive pressure on real wages and living standards. The dislocations caused by technical change and shifts in industrial concentration were overlaid by wartime shortages and food scarcities, price inflation, financial instability and post-war depression. The concurrent rise of poverty was a national phenomenon experienced in both town and country, but poverty among able-bodied farm-workers was particularly noticeable because migration towards sources of employment tended to be most common over short distances, and in villages remote from large towns or expanding centres of industry surplus labour tended to accumulate in stagnant pools. In the summers there was plenty of harvesting work and all idle hands might find work, but in winters farmers cut back their labour requirements and the surplus men again found themselves dependent on poor relief.

It will be clear to the reader that parliamentary enclosure, with its strongly regional character, could not be responsible for what became a national problem. Rural poverty, in fact, was worse in eastern and southern counties where enclosure affected only a small proportion of the farmland. In the Midlands, where enclosure was concentrated, poverty was at lower levels. Of course, large areas of the Midlands saw considerable industrial and urban growth which helped to absorb any surplus of rural labour which was created where enclosure resulted in conversion of arable to pasture. Lastly, it is worth pointing out that the agrarian riots of the post-1815

55. Notts. RO: DDSY 169/xxiii.

years, most notably the widespread Swing riots of 1830, were concentrated in East Anglia, the south-east and the south of England where there had been little or no industrial growth (outside London and its immediate surroundings), and equally little parliamentary enclosure.

In general, therefore, it is difficult to disentangle the effects on employment of enclosure from other influences of the time; but it is evident, at least, that enclosure was not a *general* cause of unemployment and poverty, though it might well have been responsible for some local distress, especially in areas away from industrial developments.

CHAPTER EIGHT

Conclusion: The Continuing Debate

As was noted in the Introduction to this volume, parliamentary enclosure has been the subject of controversy for over a hundred years. The debate continues: broadly, the difference of opinion is not so much one of ideology, between historians of the left and those of the right; rather it depends more on what weight is given, on the one hand, to the social effects – the loss and distress experienced by squatters, cottagers and small occupiers, and how extensive these effects were; and, on the other hand, to the economic benefits, in the shape of increased food production and, often, expanded rural employment at a time of an upsurge in population and rapid urbanisation.

The economic benefits were frequently very considerable, with enclosure paving the way for more rational use of farm land, improved types of farming, and the cultivation of formerly unproductive moors, heaths and marshes. In view of the rapid growth of the non-agricultural population, these changes were of great importance in producing additional food for consumption, and particularly as this was achieved with a falling proportion of the national labour force. Two words of caution are necessary here, however. First, enclosure opened the way to these advances, but they did not necessarily follow, at least not immediately. There was often a substantial time-gap between an enclosure and any major improvements in the farming of the parish in question – the nature of the soil and access to markets were important determining factors. Secondly, since parliamentary enclosure affected only a proportion of the country's land, something like a quarter of it, then it follows that the greater part of the increase in agricultural production and productivity which marked the hundred years after 1750 came from land that was already enclosed, or perhaps had never been open,

148

or in some degree from the other types of enclosure which were proceeding at the same time as parliamentary enclosure.

Similar caution is necessary in assessing the social effects. First, not all enclosures inflicted loss and distress on the poorer elements of rural society: in what was probably a small minority of instances there were significant gains for cottagers and small occupiers. When the small freeholder sold out at the time of enclosure this was not always because of the financial burden of the costs but, as we have seen, for a whole variety of reasons. Secondly, parliamentary enclosure being very much a *regional* matter – widespread in the Midlands but much less so elsewhere – it cannot be held entirely responsible for the appearance of the great social changes of the time, such as the increase in poverty and more extensive migration, which were to a large extent *national* questions. And, as we have seen, the rural unrest which was a marked feature of the later eighteenth century and early nineteenth century, and particularly of the years between 1816 and 1831, was due to a wide variety of influences.

These included the high cost of food, especially during the Napoleonic Wars; the distress which arose from the widespread depression in the economy at the end of the Wars; the failure in some areas of agricultural wages to provide an acceptable standard of living – a major factor in the Swing riots of 1830–1; and the unemployment and consequent dependence on a demeaning and demoralising system of poor relief, a condition which grew when labour stagnated in the absence of sufficient migration to towns and industrial centres. The enclosures, where they occurred, certainly added to these forces but did not necessarily constitute a major one in themselves, even in heavily enclosed districts. Enclosure, in fact, was only one element in a whole complex of factors bearing on people's living standards in a limited period which saw more rapid changes in the country's social and economic structure than had occurred over previous centuries.

Where enclosure's effects were most devastating, perhaps, was in the loss of a small but important degree of independence when petty occupiers and cottagers lost their access to commons and, with that, the livestock on which their independence was largely based. In the areas enclosed there was a gradual transformation of a poor but semi-independent peasantry into a labour force more entirely reliant on full-time employment and wages. This was the price that had to be paid for the modernisation of a significant portion of the country's agriculture. The remaining open fields, commons and wastes were seen by progressive landowners, farmers and professional experts as hindrances to more advanced farming, and with the pressures of rapid population growth and wartime food shortages there had to be change. More and more people who depended on non-agricultural incomes had to be fed, and the market mechanism made it profitable for this need to be met. The passing of the old system, therefore, was inevitable, and the pressures for change were so great that the transformation was rapid – unlike the situation in some other western European countries where the abolition of open fields was a much more gradual, catching-up process, lasting in some areas to as late as the second half of the twentieth century.

Recent work by historians continues to keep the issues of enclosure alive. In a study of 1992, based on research in the south Midlands, Professor Allen argues that the economic benefits were limited, since he sees the rise of output in English agriculture as a very long-term development, one stretching over previous centuries, to which the parliamentary enclosures contributed only marginally.[1] (It should be noted here that this is quite contrary to the view of the most recent study of the 'agricultural revolution', which puts the major increases in both output and productivity firmly in the era of parliamentary enclosure.[2])

On the social effects, Allen comes down heavily on the side of the traditional Marxist or left-wing view that people were forced out of farming and a labour surplus accumulated in the villages. This surplus, he states, found little outlet in the spread of hand trades, at least in the south Midlands region, but before the eighteenth century had helped to swell the rapid growth of London. In the period of parliamentary enclosure he finds that migration of surplus labour from the south Midlands decreased, and in the absence of sufficient outlets in hand industries and other occupations the region saw widespread seasonal unemployment.[3] He also states that the small family farm, defined as under 60 acres, was 'eliminated' in the course of the acquisition of large estates by major landowners, although his own figures show that in about 1800 nearly 30 per cent of open-field farms, and nearly 35 per cent of enclosed ones, were of 60 acres and under.[4] Allen overstates his case: the small family farm may well have declined, but it certainly was not 'eliminated',

---

1. Robert C. Allen, *Enclosure and the Yeoman: the Agricultural Development of the South Midlands, 1450–1850*, Oxford, 1992, p. 21.

2. Mark Overton, *Agricultural Revolution in England: the Transformation of the Agrarian Economy 1500–1850*, Cambridge, 1996, pp. 75–7.

3. Allen, *Enclosure and the Yeoman*, pp. 19, 241–3.   4. Ibid., pp. 14, 73–4.

and indeed a variety of market and practical considerations ensured its survival, notably the rise in demand in towns and industrial areas for the small man's specialised products.

Another recent controversial study is that of Dr J.M. Neeson on Northamptonshire.[5] In considering her views it is important to remember that Northamptonshire, with some 316,000 acres enclosed, had the highest proportion of its land affected by enclosure of any county, 50 per cent, according to Turner's figures. For the whole of England the average proportion enclosed was only 13.1 per cent, so that Northamptonshire was nearly four times over the average in its density of enclosure. Further, a very high proportion of the acreage enclosed in Northamptonshire consisted of open fields and commons; outside the Midlands, especially in northern England, enclosures were more largely of waste. In Northamptonshire, in fact, almost all the parliamentary enclosures were of open-field arable and commons – nearly 96 per cent of the total. It follows that the effects experienced in the county were not typical of enclosure more generally, and certainly not of England as a whole. And since so high a proportion of the land enclosed consisted of open-field arable and associated commons, the kind of enclosure more likely to cause disruption and possible loss to small occupiers and cottagers – and very little indeed consisted of enclosure of waste lands, which generally increased employment – it is evident that Northamptonshire is far from being a typical county so far as parliamentary enclosure is concerned. Over the whole of England, in fact, the proportion of open-field arable to all land affected by parliamentary enclosure, according to Turner, was 66 per cent.[6]

Dr Neeson's research brought her to estimate that possibly 'in many common-field villages on the eve of enclosure as many as half of the villagers were entitled to common grazing because they occupied land'. The numbers of cottages having common rights attached to them varied greatly from village to village but, in total, she believes, commoners with rights of pasture were 'perhaps half of the county population on the eve of enclosure'.[7] (It should be noted in passing that numbers of these commoners were farmers and small occupiers, while others were not farming people but

5. J.M. Neeson, *Commoners: Common Right, Enclosure and Social Change in England, 1700–1820*, Cambridge, 1993.

6. Michael Turner, *English Parliamentary Enclosure: its Historical Geography and Economic History*, Folkestone, 1950, pp. 178, 180–1, 190–1.

7. Neeson, *Commoners*, pp. 61, 64.

full-time or part-time industrial workers, village craftsmen, traders and innkeepers who occupied cottages which possessed common rights.) In some instances the resources of the common might be of considerable value but in others over-stocking was a problem and stinting might make it more difficult for cottagers to use the common for their beasts.[8] The major factors in creating a different post-enclosure situation were, first, the extent to which holdings were consolidated before enclosure, and, secondly, the disappearance of the majority of commons. There was a decline in numbers of small occupiers, which was most marked among those with holdings of between 5 and 25 acres.[9]

In twenty-three of Northamptonshire's unenclosed parishes between 22 and 73 per cent of the population held land as owners or occupiers in 1778–1815, although wider evidence suggests that occupiers of 50 acres or less usually held between them no more than about a quarter or a third of all the land in open-field parishes. Already, however, the large farm had made its appearance, well before enclosure.[10] Neeson concludes that in most Northamptonshire villages enclosure 'destroyed the old peasant economy', with a large number of the small owners selling land and cottagers losing that access to the commons which was a mainstay of their old way of life.[11]

There must be an assumption that the changes brought about by enclosure in Northamptonshire occurred in other heavily enclosed Midland counties, though conditions certainly varied from place to place, depending mainly on the size and usefulness of the commons and the availability of waste land. Outside the Midlands the type of village community drawn by Neeson did not exist to any considerable extent. And even in the Midlands many of the traditional open-field communities had already disappeared before parliamentary enclosure, in some cases a very long time before. Turning Neeson's generalisation around, even in Northamptonshire a half of the population had no access to commons before enclosure. And of course not all the commons, even in Northamptonshire, would have possessed the multifarious resources that Neeson describes. Lastly, there is the important point that as the population increased after 1750, in Northamptonshire as elsewhere, the proportion of villagers having access to land of any sort despite some division of common rights would necessarily have diminished.

8. Ibid., pp. 87–90.   9. Ibid., pp. 228, 234.
10. Ibid., pp. 205, 305, 307–8.   11. Ibid., p. 223.

Agrarian reform, however painful, was essential for the modernisation of farming and expansion of the food supply in an era of rising prices and acute shortages.

There is, of course, the question of whether there had to be disruption of traditional communities. Could not reform have been carried out while preserving the property and rights of small men? Could not the sense of betrayal emphasised by Neeson[12] have been assuaged, if not totally avoided, if more had been done to preserve customary as well as legal rights, and the tradition of looking to the ruling classes for protection had not been broken?

The opposition to enclosure, and the severe unrest to which it sometimes gave rise, it might be thought, should have inhibited landowners, clergy and farmers from pushing their legal claims too far; or better still, they might have adopted measures to ensure the preservation of widespread access to land. But those having the larger interests, anxious to see enclosure pay, usually took no steps to make the process more readily acceptable to small owners and occupiers, and found the taking in and cultivation of 'improvable' commons one of the main attractions of the project. The contemporary agricultural experts, too, egged them on: most notably Arthur Young, with his contempt for the supposed inefficiency of small farms and his attacks on the 'Goths and Vandals' of the open fields.[13]

In defence of the experts, the old way of farming, it must be remembered, had many weaknesses. The necessary fallowing of a substantial proportion of the arable land placed a limit on output, while communal restrictions circumscribed the progress that could be made by the more enterprising farmers. The pasture was often insufficient for all the stock that villagers wanted to keep, and periodically disease wreaked havoc among animals grazed in common. Further, although access to the land for keeping a cow or horse was vital to many of the village poor, the importance of the common for this purpose may be exaggerated, even if it was extensive in area. It has to be remembered that numbers of commons were of very little value for grazing – 'all either heath or rushes', as an observer noted on a visit to Oxfordshire in 1775.[14] Again, even the rights to a good common might be of limited value where other

12. Ibid., p. 327.

13. William Marshall, *Review of Reports to the Board of Agriculture*, York, 1808–18, I, p. 370; Arthur Young, *Eastern Tour*, 1771, II, pp. 161–2: Arthur Young, *General View of Oxfordshire*, 1809, pp. 35–6.

14. James L. Clifford, ed., *Dr Campbell's Diary of a Visit to England in 1775*, Cambridge, 1947, p. 42.

pasture was plentiful and of better quality, and arable farming was not of major importance. The gathering of fuel from the common was costly in terms of the cottager's time and energy. He and his wife and children might well be better employed in tending crops or stock on a little rented land and buying their fuel from woodmen, than in walking a long distance to bring home a fallen bough, a load of gorse or a bundle of twigs.

Undoubtedly the eagerness to enclose, especially in the period of rising prices in the later eighteenth century and the Napoleonic Wars, together with the primacy given to legal rights to property, over-rode any scruples that the major interests might have had over the consequences for the poorer elements of the village community. These poorer elements, it should be recalled, included not only the cottagers in those villages mainly concerned with farming but also considerable numbers of dairymen, craftsmen and petty traders whose livelihood depended to a considerable or even crucial extent on access to the fields and commons.[15] The hastening of profitable reform was fuelled also by contemporary morality. Property-owners were likely to agree with those who saw the commons as a cause of idleness and fecklessness, a means of enabling the poor to live without the discipline of regular full-time work. Some went beyond this and thought that the commons encouraged not merely idleness but also dissipation and crime.

Not all took this view, however. Arthur Young in his later years was appalled to find how the loss of access to land had increased poverty and given rise to an outraged sense of legalised dispossession among the village poor. He was impressed by the pride in ownership and the independence that the possession of a little piece of land, or even of just a single cow, could bring. In a pamphlet published in 1801 he argued 'that nothing tends so strongly to give the poor industrious and frugal habits as the prospect of acquiring, or the hope of preserving land'. He proposed that in future enclosures of waste, sufficient land should be set aside to enable cottagers to maintain a cow, and he mentioned some examples where provision had been made in line with his views. He recommended also that an allotment should be made to the parish for the purpose of accommodating families who were willing to accept land in lieu of receiving poor relief.[16]

15. J.M. Martin, 'Village Traders and the Emergence of a Proletariat in South Warwickshire 1750–1861', *Agricultural History Review*, XXXII, 1984, pp. 180, 187.

16. Arthur Young, *An Inquiry into the Propriety of Applying Wastes to the Better Maintenance and Support of the Poor*, Bury St Edmunds, 1801, pp. 25–7.

Indeed, much of the early nineteenth-century concern with providing cottagers with land arose from the burden of rising poor
rates. In 1813 Young noted some instances in Lincolnshire where
large proprietors had provided cottagers with land to keep them off
the poor rates: at Freiston, near Boston, for example, a Mr Linton
gave his labourers sufficient land to keep a cow, a pig and a few
sheep – about 4 acres of 'tolerably good' land. This landowner's
father and grandfather had introduced and first practised this policy. At Swinhope, a few miles from Market Rasen, Mr Allington's
regular labourers had cows, and if they could not find the money
to buy one then the landlord provided it, while on the Duke of
Ancaster's estate the labourers had land of from 3 to 8 acres, and
some as much as 14 or 15 acres, and 'they are enabled to bring
up their families without the aid of the parish'.[17] Elsewhere, Thomas
Babington provided twenty-six cottagers and village tradesmen with
sufficient land to keep one to three cows each and raise vegetables
for the family. He noted that the wives and daughters did most of
the milking and managing of the cows so that the husbands were
not prevented from pursuing their regular employment, except for
about a week at hay harvest and a few days at other times.[18]

There were other landowners who took steps to provide cottagers
with land sufficient for cows, most notably perhaps Earl Winchelsea,
but for the most part the motive inspiring them was to find an
answer to rising poor rates rather than to help those dispossessed
by enclosure. Moreover, although when Young put forward his
ideas in 1801 there were numerous enclosures of waste going forward, in other enclosures little waste was available even had there
been a desire to provide for the poor. And, of course, with the rising
population landlords would have found it difficult or impossible to
give land to more than a small fraction of the growing village community. As Professor Chambers remarked over forty years ago,

> in his enthusiasm for the growing 'cow-ocracy' of Lincolnshire, Arthur
> Young unwittingly let a portentous cat out of his rather hastily packed
> bag when he wrote that as a result, the 'population increases so that
> pigs and children fill every quarter. . . . The women, however, are
> very lazy; they do nothing but bring children and eat cake.'[19]

17. Arthur Young, *General View of Lincolnshire*, 1808, pp. 465–8.
18. Arthur Young, ed., *Annals of Agriculture*, XLIV, 1806, pp. 101–3.
19. J.D. Chambers, 'Enclosure and Labour Supply in the Industrial Revolution',
Economic History Review, 2nd ser., V, 3, 1953, p. 337, quoting Young, *General View*,
1808, p. 462.

There were other problems too. Even the provision of veget-
able allotments, which developed in the early nineteenth century
largely at the instance of country parsons like the Revd Stephen
Demainbray of Broad Somerford in Wiltshire, ran into the opposition of farmers who objected to their men gaining even this slight
degree of independence.

Although there were significant exceptions, landowners in general failed to provide cottagers with land. It is true that in a number
of enclosures the Commissioners were authorised to allocate the
cottagers' allotments in one piece so that cows (or crops) could be
raised collectively. In some enclosures, too, the Commissioners were
instructed to allocate land to trustees, the income from the land to
be used to provide fuel for the poor. Alternatively, land was sometimes set aside for cottagers to gather the fuel for themselves. But
the allotments, where they were made, were not always adequate
for the purpose.

Under the influence of the rising market for agricultural produce, the prospect of higher farmers' profits and increased rents
for landowners, it proved impossible to leave the old system untouched. Its supposed inefficiencies, wasted resources and low rents
stood out as disfiguring blots when agriculture was generally advanc-
ing, and progress and reform were constantly on the lips of the
large propertied interests. But in carrying out the reforms concern
for small occupiers and cottagers was often lacking, and even the
compensation awarded to the legitimate claimants of common rights,
while legally fair perhaps, was not a true equivalent of access to
an open common, however limited its resources might be. There
can be but little doubt that for many of the rural poor enclosure
enforced an unwelcome transformation in their way of life, in their
personal prospects, and their standard of comfort. Nevertheless,
the matter should not be judged in the light of late twentieth-
century morality. There were very many honest, God-fearing members of the propertied classes who had come to believe that it was
morally better for the poor themselves to have to work in regular
employment, to follow a disciplined if frugal existence, than to
continue living in the insidious sloth and contemptible torpor
induced by the availability of a little free grazing, the keeping of a
half-starved cow, and the meagre rewards of the hours spent in
collecting what was at best inferior fuel for the hearth.

It is true that a great number of small cultivators, petty
husbandmen as they were called, had disappeared before parliamentary enclosure, in some areas long before. Some of those who

were freeholders were bought out by large landowners with an eye
to paving the way for an eventual enclosure, whether by agreement
or, later, by Act of Parliament. Those who held their land by a lease
for three lives found their landlords refusing to renew the lives as
they fell in, so that eventually they became tenants on an annual
basis or for terms of years. Other small men, freeholders and tenants, succumbed because the natural conditions of their district,
or the markets of the time, were unfavourable to their survival. In
the Cotswolds, for example, small cultivators declined in the later
seventeenth century, though there was no great extent of enclosure
in the district at that period. In the open sheep-and-corn farming
districts of Wiltshire there was a great increase in the numbers
of very small occupiers and landless people; at the same time a
decline occurred also in the numbers of medium-size holdings
suitable for family farms, which was due to the lower proportional
costs of the large farms. In the enclosures of the parliamentary era
small men again declined, but consolidation of holdings was already
taking place in the open fields before enclosure, and the enclosures therefore 'only accelerated an existing tendency'.[20]

Another example of the earlier changes that arose before enclosure comes from an entirely different area, that of the lake counties.
Historians of Cumberland and Westmorland conclude that enclosure accelerated a process of decline among the yeomen farmers
which had begun before enclosure on any large scale had even
started. The resulting increase in the size of the farming unit generally proved an improvement in economic terms, as was also the
introduction of tenures which allowed landlords to select tenant
farmers for their skill and character. But as the commons disappeared some local observers held it unfortunate that small farmers
and poor labourers could no longer keep their livestock as before.[21]
More generally, it is true that right across the country the landless
cottager had appeared and was commonplace well before the onset
of parliamentary enclosure.

It is worth pointing out that most of the changes brought in by
the parliamentary enclosure movement were spread over a period
of some seventy-five years: a much longer time still if one goes back
to the earliest eighteenth-century Acts and forward to the completion of the process by the General Enclosure Acts of the nineteenth

20. *Victoria County History of Wiltshire*, IV, ed. Elizabeth Crittall, 1959; E. Kerridge,
'Agriculture c.1500–c.1793, pp. 46, 47, 49; R. Molland, 'Agriculture 1793–1870', p. 67.
21. C.M.L. Bouch and G.P. Jones, *The Lake Counties, 1500–1830*, Manchester,
1961, pp. 237, 238–9.

century. In most other parts of western Europe agricultural reform was even more gradual. But in Russia after 1920, however, and later in eastern Europe, the pressure for reform of an extremely backward agricultural economy resulted in drastic revolution forced through by a ruthless state machine in a matter of a very few decades, resulting in untold misery, loss, destitution and famine on a vast scale. By such standards, it might be argued, the English parliamentary enclosures were relatively painless, even if the way of life of thousands of commoners was transformed by them.

One last point remains to be reiterated. Parliamentary enclosure was essentially a regional experience, affecting some districts heavily, other lightly, or not at all. One should not generalise in broad national terms on a matter that was so intrinsically regional. Even in the most heavily enclosed counties a substantial part of the farm land was not affected because it was already enclosed. Furthermore, many of the parishes enclosed by private Act were very little affected: the Act might deal with only a small surviving area of open fields and commons left behind by earlier enclosure, or perhaps merely gave legal standing to an enclosure already carried out by agreement. That the effects varied greatly between county and county, between district and district within counties, and between parish and parish, must enforce caution in framing general judgments of what was so evidently a highly complex process, varying geographically, and having effects which, if often painful or disastrous for many, were generally beneficial in economic terms, and even, in not a few instances, in social terms also.

Maps

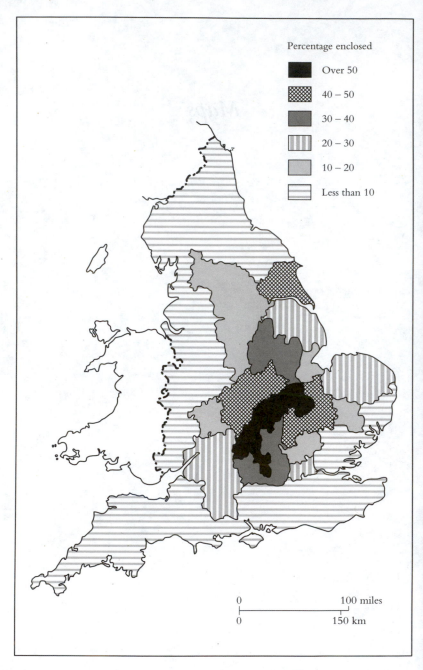

Percentage enclosed

	Over 50
	40 – 50
	30 – 40
	20 – 30
	10 – 20
	Less than 10

0   100 miles
0   150 km

Map 1   Density of parliamentary enclosure of open-field arable in England.
Source: Reproduced from Michael Turner, *English Parliamentary Enclosure: Its Historical Geography and Economic History*, Folkestone, 1980 by kind permission of Dawson UK Ltd.

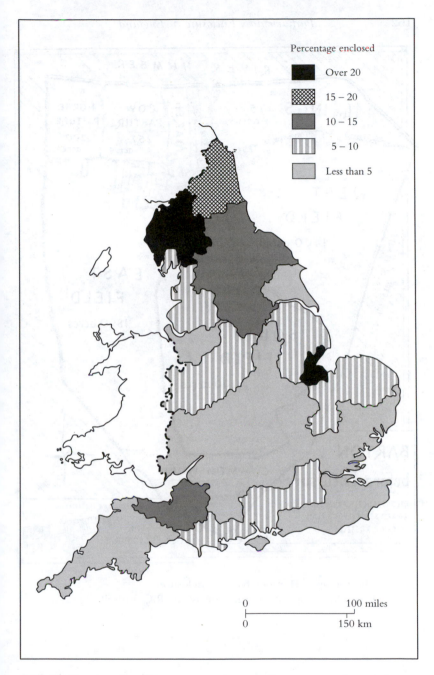

Map 2   Density of parliamentary enclosure of common and waste in England.
Source: Reproduced from Michael Turner, *English Parliamentary Enclosure: Its Historical Geography and Economic History*, Folkestone, 1980 by kind permission of Dawson UK Ltd.

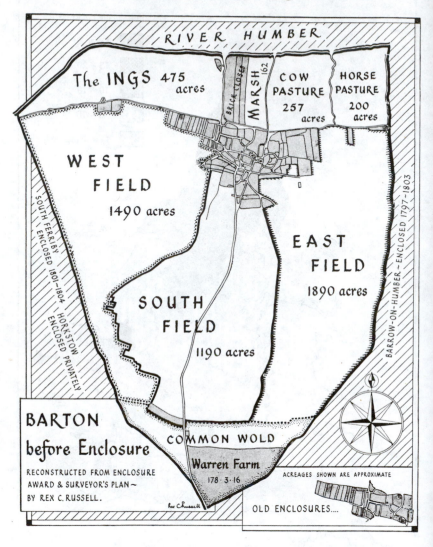

Map 3   Barton-upon-Humber before enclosure.
Source: Reproduced by kind permission of Mr R.C. Russell.

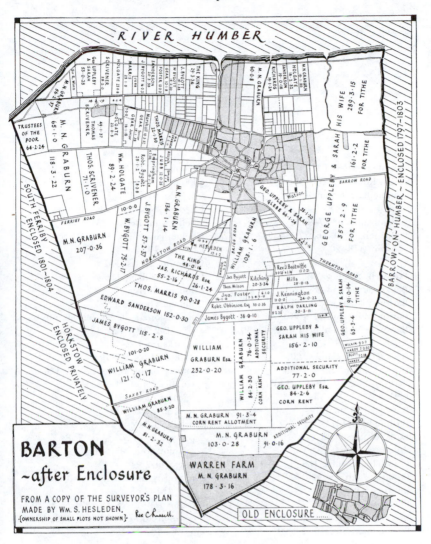

Map 4   Barton-upon-Humber after enclosure.
Source: Reproduced by kind permission of Mr R.C. Russell.

Index